JAN - - 2011

THIS IS NO LON
OF THE SEATTLE PUBLIC LIBRARY

D0436434

CONSTITUTIONAL
AMENDMENTS
BEYOND THE BILL OF RIGHTS

# Amendment XIV
# Citizenship for All

# Other Books of Related Interest

**Opposing Viewpoints Series**

Civil Liberties

Feminism

Race Relations

Work

Working Women

**Current Controversies Series**

Civil Liberties

Extremist Groups

Feminism

Human Rights

CONSTITUTIONAL
AMENDMENTS
BEYOND THE BILL OF RIGHTS

# Amendment XIV
# Citizenship for All

*Jeff Hay, Book Editor*

**GREENHAVEN PRESS**
*A part of Gale, Cengage Learning*

GALE
CENGAGE Learning™

Detroit • New York • San Francisco • New Haven, Conn • Waterville, Maine • London

Christine Nasso, *Publisher*
Elizabeth Des Chenes, *Managing Editor*

© 2009 Greenhaven Press, a part of Gale, Cengage Learning.

Gale and Greenhaven Press are registered trademarks used herein under license.

*For more information, contact:*
Greenhaven Press
27500 Drake Rd.
Farmington Hills, MI 48331-3535
Or you can visit our Internet site at gale.cengage.com

**ALL RIGHTS RESERVED.**
No part of this work covered by the copyright herein may be reproduced, transmitted, stored, or used in any form or by any means graphic, electronic, or mechanical, including but not limited to photocopying, recording, scanning, digitizing, taping, Web distribution, information networks, or information storage and retrieval systems, except as permitted under Section 107 or 108 of the 1976 United States Copyright Act, without the prior written permission of the publisher.

For product information and technology assistance, contact us at

Gale Customer Support, 1-800-877-4253
For permission to use material from this text or product, submit all requests online at www.cengage.com/permissions

Further permissions questions can be emailed to permissionrequest@cengage.com

Articles in Greenhaven Press anthologies are often edited for length to meet page requirements. In addition, original titles of these works are changed to clearly present the main thesis and to explicitly indicate the author's opinion. Every effort is made to ensure that Greenhaven Press accurately reflects the original intent of the authors. Every effort has been made to trace the owners of copyrighted material.

Cover photograph © Morton Beebe/Corbis.

**LIBRARY OF CONGRESS CATALOGING-IN-PUBLICATION DATA**

Amendment XIV : citizenship for all / Jeff Hay, book editor.
    p. cm. -- (Constitutional amendments)
  Includes bibliographical references and index.
  ISBN-13: 978-0-7377-4124-7 (hardcover)
  1. Citizenship--United States. 2. Citizenship--United States--History. 3. United States. Constitution. 14th Amendment. 4. African Americans--Civil rights.
5. Immigrants--Civil rights--United States. I. Hay, Jeff. II. Title: Amendment 14. III. Title: Amendment Fourteen.
  KF4700.A96 2009
  342.7308'3--dc22
                                   2008031773

Printed in the United States of America
1 2 3 4 5 6 7 12 11 10 09 08

# Contents

## Chapter 1: Historical Background on the Fourteenth Amendment

*Akhil Reed Amar*

A Constitutional scholar examines how the Fourteenth Amendment overturned the Supreme Court's Dred Scott decision of 1857, which had declared that black people could never be full citizens of the United States and which was one of the important factors inspiring the American Civil War of 1861 to 1865.

*Kenneth L. Karst*

A legal scholar illustrates how the effort to ensure that all Americans were citizens was challenged by attempts to restrict the freedoms of African Americans in Southern states after the Civil War.

*James F. Wilson*

In a congressional debate, a senator from Iowa argues that the Fourteenth Amendment reinforces the U.S. Constitution as well as long-standing legal and political traditions.

# Chapter 2: Testing the Fourteenth Amendment's Citizenship Clause

# Amendment XIV: Citizenship for All

> *"Today's Constitution is a realistic document of freedom only because of several corrective amendments. Those amendments speak to a sense of decency and fairness."*
>
> *Thurgood Marshall*

While the U.S. Constitution forms the backbone of American democracy, the amendments make the Constitution a living, ever-evolving document. Interpretation and analysis of the Constitution inform lively debate in every branch of government, as well as among students, scholars, and all other citizens, and views on various articles of the Constitution have changed over the generations. Formally altering the Constitution, however, can happen only through the amendment process. The Greenhaven Press series The Bill of Rights examines the first ten amendments to the Constitution. Constitutional Amendments: Beyond the Bill of Rights continues the exploration, addressing key amendments ratified since 1791.

The process of amending the Constitution is painstaking. While other options are available, the method used for nearly every amendment begins with a congressional bill that must pass both the Senate and the House of Representatives by a two-thirds majority. Then the amendment must be ratified by three-quarters of the states. Many amendments have been proposed since the Bill of Rights was adopted in 1791, but only seventeen have been ratified.

It may be difficult to imagine a United States where women and African Americans are prohibited from voting, where the federal government allows one human being to enslave another, or where some citizens are denied equal protection under the law. While many of our most fundamental liberties are protected by the Bill of Rights, the amendments that followed have significantly broadened and enhanced the rights of American citizens. Such rights may be taken for granted today, but when the amendments were ratified, many were considered groundbreaking and proved to be explosively controversial.

Each volume in Constitutional Amendments provides an in-depth exploration of an amendment and its impact through primary and secondary sources, both historical and contemporary. Primary sources include landmark Supreme Court rulings, speeches by prominent experts, and newspaper editorials. Secondary sources include historical analyses, law journal articles, book excerpts, and magazine articles. Each volume first presents the historical background of the amendment, creating a colorful picture of the circumstances surrounding the amendment's passage: the campaigns to sway public opinion, the congressional debates, and the struggle for ratification. Next, each volume examines the ways the court system has been used to test the validity of the amendment and addresses the ramifications of the amendment's passage. The final chapter of each volume presents viewpoints that explore current controversies and debates relating to ways in which the amendment affects our everyday lives.

Numerous features are included in each Constitutional Amendments volume:

- An originally written introduction presents a concise yet thorough overview of the amendment.

- A chronology provides historical context by describing key events, organizations, and people relating to the ratification of the amendment, subsequent court cases, and the impact of the amendment.

- An annotated table of contents offers an at-a-glance summary of each primary and secondary source essay included in the volume.

- The complete text of the amendment, followed by a "plain English" explanation, brings the amendment into clear focus for students and other readers.

- Graphs, charts, tables, and maps enhance the text.

- A list of all twenty-seven Constitutional Amendments offers quick reference.

- An annotated list of court cases relevant to the amendment broadens the reader's understanding of the judiciary's role in interpreting the Constitution.

- A bibliography of books, periodicals, and Web sites aids readers in further research.

- A detailed subject index allows readers to quickly find the information they need.

With the aid of this series, students and other researchers will become better informed of their rights and responsibilities as American citizens. Constitutional Amendments: Beyond the Bill of Rights examines the roots of American democracy, bringing to life the ways the Constitution has evolved and how it has impacted this nation's history.

# Amendment Text and Explanation

## The Fourteenth Amendment to the United States Constitution

*Passed by Congress June 13, 1866. Ratified July 9, 1868.*

**Note**: Article I, Section 2, of the Constitution was modified by Section 2 of the Fourteenth Amendment.

**Section 1.** All persons born or naturalized in the United States, and subject to the jurisdiction thereof, are citizens of the United States and of the State wherein they reside. No State shall make or enforce any law which shall abridge the privileges or immunities of citizens of the United States; nor shall any State deprive any person of life, liberty, or property, without due process of law; nor deny to any person within its jurisdiction the equal protection of the laws.

**Section 2.** Representatives shall be apportioned among the several States according to their respective numbers, counting the whole number of persons in each State, excluding Indians not taxed. But when the right to vote at any election for the choice of electors for President and Vice-President of the United States, Representatives in Congress, the Executive and Judicial officers of a State, or the members of the Legislature thereof, is denied to any of the male inhabitants of such State, being twenty-one years of age*, and citizens of the United States, or in any way abridged, except for participation in rebellion, or other crime, the basis of representation therein shall be reduced in the proportion which the number of such male citizens shall bear to the whole number of male citizens twenty-one years of age in such State.

**Section 3.** No person shall be a Senator or Representative in Congress, or elector of President and Vice-President, or

* *Changed [to eighteen years of age] by Section 1 of the Twenty-sixth Amendment.*

hold any office, civil or military, under the United States, or under any State, who, having previously taken an oath, as a member of Congress, or as an officer of the United States, or as a member of any State legislature, or as an executive or judicial officer of any State, to support the Constitution of the United States, shall have engaged in insurrection or rebellion against the same, or given aid or comfort to the enemies thereof. But Congress may by a vote of two-thirds of each House, remove such disability.

**Section 4.** The validity of the public debt of the United States, authorized by law, including debts incurred for payment of pensions and bounties for services in suppressing insurrection or rebellion, shall not be questioned. But neither the United States nor any State shall assume or pay any debt or obligation incurred in aid of insurrection or rebellion against the United States, or any claim for the loss or emancipation of any slave; but all such debts, obligations and claims shall be held illegal and void.

**Section 5.** The Congress shall have the power to enforce, by appropriate legislation, the provisions of this article.

# Explanation

The heart of the Fourteenth Amendment to the Constitution is Section 1, which introduced the notions of birthright citizenship, the right of all citizens to due process of law, and the principle of equal protection under the law for all Americans. The first of these, and the subject of this volume, was a constitutional guarantee that all people born on U.S. soil were citizens of the country. This would remain true even if one's parents were born elsewhere. Section 1 also refers to "naturalized" citizens. These are people, generally immigrants, who have become U.S. citizens through the bureaucratic process of naturalization, which has taken many forms but tends to be reasonably clear in any given era. Modern-day newscasts often cover the naturalization ceremonies in which immigrants, having fulfilled various requirements, take oaths of allegiance to the United States and thereby become naturalized U.S. citizens.

Section 1 also refines the relationship between the U.S. federal government and those of the individual states. It asserts that both native-born and naturalized Americans are citizens of both the nation and of the states where they live. In this manner the Amendment implies that the individual states cannot enact citizenship rules that differ widely from those established by the federal government. Furthermore, Section 1 asserts, all citizens shall have the same rights to due process of law and equal protection that the federal government guarantees. No individual state might take away, for example, the ability of a citizen to the right of trial by a jury of his or her peers if he or she is indicted for a crime, an example of due process, or to be tried under the assumption that he or she is "innocent until proven guilty." All citizens, whether native-born or naturalized, also should be free to enjoy protections equally, from such dangers as arbitrary arrest or imprisonment. No individual state, again, would now be free to single out particular individuals or groups for such treatment. As long as one was a U.S. citizen, one's "privileges and immunities" were now constitutionally guaranteed.

Sections 2, 3, and 4 of the Fourteenth Amendment reflect the efforts of its proponents to extend and refine Reconstruction, the rebuilding of the American Union after the devastation of the Civil War. Section 2 is mostly concerned with the representation of the states in the U.S. House of Representatives, where the number of each state's representatives depends on that state's voting population. Notably, in the years after the Civil War, some states would find their voting population greatly increased with the expansion of full citizenship rights to free blacks and former slaves. The right to vote in those days was, however, restricted to men aged twenty-one years or over. It took a much later constitutional amendment to extend the right to vote to women. Section 2, meanwhile, did recognize that the states might restrict the right to vote in certain circumstances or for local elections, and that in that case the arithmetic by which the number of representatives were chosen might change.

Section 3 of the Fourteenth Amendment is designed to assure that American officials who have actively engaged in or supported a rebellion against the United States can be prohibited from serving as American officials in the future. These prohibitions include both federal and state offices as well as the U.S. military. They also include the office of "elector," which here, as in Section 2, refers to those officials who serve the states in the Electoral College that, following elections, selects a president every four years. The language of Section 3 provides Congress with the ability to lift these prohibitions with certain conditions.

Section 4 of the Fourteenth Amendment asserts that the post–Civil War government will not be responsible for any public debts incurred by the rebellious Southern states in the process of fighting against the Union. Likewise, it gives the federal government the ability to reject any claim for compensation that might be made by the former owners of freed slaves who, in the years before they were freed, were legally considered property.

In Section 5 Congress reserves the right to enforce the Fourteenth Amendment through its lawmaking power.

*Because the Fourteenth Amendment has many distinct provisions, no single book in this series can cover all of them. This book covers only the Citizenship Clause—that is, the first clause of Section 1.*

# Introduction

The United States of America was formed from an original collection of thirteen colonies in the 1770s and 1780s. These colonies, which ranged from Vermont in the north to Georgia in the south, originally came into being as separate entities. Each had its own local government, its own economy, and its own relationship with the mother country, Great Britain. It was only when the residents of these colonies realized that they had common interests and common grievances that they came together to, first, fight the successful American Revolution and, second, devise a constitution that created a union of thirteen states that was fully independent from Britain. As the nineteenth century progressed, and as American interests expanded westward, new states were added to the union. Indeed, by the time the Civil War began in 1861, there were thirty-four of these "United States." And while each sent representatives to the national government based in Washington, D.C., each also maintained a sense of its independence from that government. One reflection of that sense of independence was the right to choose who were to be true citizens of the states and how such citizenship was to be determined. By 1789 the U.S. Constitution was ratified by all thirteen original states, and by 1861 twelve amendments had been added to it. The document, however, had yet to clarify the right of national citizenship in relation to the right of citizenship in one of the states.

America's Civil War was fought over the complicated interrelationships between the national government and the states, specifically over states' rights. Most Southern states claimed that they had the right to maintain the institution of slavery and that the national government could not enact antislavery laws that overrode the laws of the states. Adding fuel to the flames were the facts that many Northern states were vehemently opposed to slavery and that, as new territories were added to the union, controversies arose over whether they might be permitted to maintain slavery. Ready to defend their perception of states' rights, many Southern states broke away from the union, beginning with South Carolina in December 1860. In time, eleven states seceded from the American union and formed a new one, which they called the Confederate States of America. Abraham Lincoln, inaugurated as president in March 1861, insisted that such measures were unconstitutional. Both sides took up arms and began a four-year conflict that devastated much of the old South and left more than 600,000 soldiers dead. Confederate leaders, facing defeat, finally surrendered to their Union counterparts in April 1965. Lincoln's Emancipation Proclamation of 1863, in which he declared that all slaves were free people, could now be enforced throughout a restored but badly scarred American Union.

The Fourteenth Amendment to the U.S. Constitution was the second of three so-called Restoration Amendments, the others being the Thirteenth and Fifteenth. They were proposed and ratified during the early years of America's Restoration era, when the nation's leaders tried to heal the wounds of the Civil War and create or change institutions in ways that would prevent any similar struggles in the future. Many of the guiding figures in the first years of Restoration were senators and congressmen who belonged to the so-called Radical wing of the Republican Party, men such as Thaddeus Stevens of Pennsylvania and Charles Sumner of Massachusetts. These Radical Republicans lacked much sympathy for the formerly rebellious Southern states and the rights that they claimed, and they generally insisted that the federal government had the power to enact and enforce laws that superseded states' rights.

Among the major issues of Reconstruction was the citizenship status of former slaves and of African Americans in general (there had been communities of free blacks since the days of the thirteen colonies). In the Dred Scott case of 1857, the U.S. Supreme Court had determined that people of African background could not be citizens of the nation. The Radicals believed that the decision, one of the Supreme Court's most controversial ever and one of the flashpoints that led to the Civil War, had to be reversed. Another challenge was the passage of bodies of so-called Black Codes in many of the states of the former Confederacy. These greatly restricted the rights of former slaves, going so far in many cases as denying them the right to vote.

In early 1866, and in the face of opposition from politicians sympathetic to the Southern states, the Radical Republicans pushed through Congress a Civil Rights Act. It laid out specific rights that African Americans would have, such as the right to enter into contracts or to give evidence in court. But the Act also asserted that African Americans were full citizens of the United States. To drive the point home, the Act's writers included language that made it plain that the basis for this citizenship was the simple fact of having been born on American soil. President Andrew Johnson, who had succeeded Lincoln after his assassination in 1865, vetoed the Act. But his Radical counterparts in Congress overrode the veto, and it became law.

Meanwhile, the states ratified the Thirteenth Amendment to the U.S. Constitution in 1865. This, the first of the Reconstruction Amendments, banned slavery in the United States. In so doing it completed the work of Lincoln's Emancipation Proclamation by ensuring that slavery was now constitutionally banned. Since the Constitution of the United States is the basis for not only national but state legislation, the Thirteenth Amendment ensured that no individual state could revive slavery. Its fairly rapid ratification also amounted to an assertion of federal over state authority.

Neither the Thirteenth Amendment nor the 1866 Civil Rights Act overturned the Dred Scott decision, nor did they automatically end the Black Codes. In June 1866, after debate on the matter had already begun, congressional leaders proposed a Fourteenth Amendment to the Constitution that would have the effect of doing so. Indeed, its framers hoped that the Amendment would make it impossible for the Supreme Court to declare the Civil Rights Act of 1866 unconstitutional. In the House of Representatives' initial debates over the proposed amendment, Radical Republican John Bingham of Ohio proclaimed that "It is provided in the Constitution, in the first place, that 'this Constitution,' the whole of it, not a part of it, 'shall be the supreme law of the land.' Supreme from the Penobscot [River] in the farthest east, to the remotest west where rolls the Oregon [River] . . . ."

Ratification of the Fourteenth Amendment required that it be approved by twenty-eight of the thirty-seven states that were part of the United States in the late 1860s, or three-quarters of the total. The process took two years, and it remains controversial. Some historians assert that it was advanced by a Reconstruction Congress, the Thirty-ninth, that did not include representatives from some of the former Confederate states, and that pressure was strong for some of those states to ratify it if they hoped to regain full admission to the union. Some who objected to the Amendment did so on the grounds that it amounted to an unconstitutional expansion of federal power over the states. Nevertheless, a twenty-eighth state, ironically South Carolina, ratified it in July 1868, and the Fourteenth Amendment, therefore, was added to the Constitution. Most of the remaining nine states ratified it later, although the move was mostly symbolic since the Amendment was in place already. Meanwhile, the third of the Reconstruction Amendments, the Fifteenth, was ratified in February 1870. It assured that no American could be denied the right to vote based on his ethnic background or on any previous status as a slave.

By the 1880s controversies over the Fourteenth Amendment's citizenship clause had flared up. Indeed, by then the ethnic makeup of the United States was beginning to change in ways unforeseen by the Amendment's authors, whose main concern was ensuring the citizenship status of former slaves. At issue now, by contrast, was the citizenship status of the children of immigrants from China. Uncomfortable with the cultural differences that Chinese people seemed to represent, Congress passed the Chinese Exclusion Act in 1882. It made it impossible for Chinese immigrants to become fully naturalized citizens. However, such new legislation could do nothing about the native-born children of such immigrants. The citizenship clause guaranteed that these children were U.S. citizens provided they were born on American soil. The Supreme Court confirmed this principle of birthright citizenship in its *United States v. Wong Kim Ark* decision of 1898. The decision became an important precedent for later challenges to the notion of citizenship by birth.

Meanwhile, the ethnic makeup of the nation continued to grow more diverse as waves of immigrants from southern and eastern Europe and from Japan arrived on American shores in the last decades of the nineteenth century and first decades of the twentieth. Few questioned whether the native-born children of such immigrants were citizens. The Fourteenth Amendment's citizenship clause continued to do its work in enabling America's "melting pot" to turn new immigrant generations into citizens. Indeed, even during World War II (1939–1945), the local-born children of Japanese immigrants never had their citizenship questioned in any legal sense. This remained true even though many of these Nisei (second-generation Japanese immigrants) were, with their parents, confined to relocation camps in the western United States for fear that elements among them might be pro-Japanese saboteurs or agents or that they might be in danger from angry local populations in coastal cities.

In the decades after World War II, the citizenship clause began to face new challenges. One was whether native-born or naturalized U.S. citizens could have their citizenship taken away. In two important cases, the Supreme Court delivered contradictory decisions. In the first of these cases, *Perez. v. Brownell*, decided in 1958, the Court determined that the plaintiff had effectively forfeited his citizenship by voting in a foreign election and taking other actions that indicated his "intent" was to live under the laws of a foreign country. The U.S. Congress, the Court affirmed, had the right to withdraw citizenship in certain circumstances. This decision was over-turned in 1967's *Afroyim v. Rusk* case. In that case, a natural-ized citizen who had also voted in a foreign election chal-lenged the removal of his citizenship. This time the Supreme Court decided that Congress did not have the right to with-draw someone's citizenship. The Fourteenth Amendment's guarantees superseded such rights.

The *Afroyim* decision, however, opened the door to yet an-other challenge to the Fourteenth Amendment's citizenship clause. In recent decades a number of countries have made it possible for people to maintain dual citizenship, a status that in the past was relatively rare. Other countries, of course, have their own citizenship requirements, and these might have little to do with place of birth. They might, for instance, be based on a person's ancestry or other factors. Combining these rights with the Fourteenth Amendment's guarantees has enabled a growing number of people to maintain dual citizenship. The Mexican government, for example, allows children born to Mexican citizens to claim such citizenship for themselves no matter where they live or whether they are naturalized or native-born U.S. citizens. Because the *Afroyim* decision and the legal and cultural stature of the U.S. Constitution make it difficult for a U.S. citizen to have his or her rights removed, the number of those who claim dual citizenship is likely to grow, especially since some 50 percent of the world's nations recognize the principle of dual citizenship. The debate about whether the sweeping guarantees in the Fourteenth Amendment should be reduced has been fueled by recent examples of American citizens who have taken up arms in defense of foreign governments.

Another source of heated debate about birthright citizenship in recent years has been the issue of illegal immigrants and their native-born children. Indeed, in some years, experts estimate, more than one million illegal immigrants have come into the United States. Some of them have children on U.S. soil who, under the guarantees of the citizenship clause, are U.S. citizens regardless of the status of their parents and are therefore granted the rights and privileges of all other Americans. Critics of this phenomenon have used the term "anchor babies" to refer to these children, implying that some illegal immigrants purposefully have children in the United States in search of certain benefits. These include access to public education and health care as well as welfare benefits. They also might include the hope that these "anchors" will make it more likely that their parents can obtain citizenship. In the minds of these critics, illegal immigrants who have such children are taking unfair advantage of the Fourteenth Amendment's guarantees. They suggest that the Fourteenth Amendment can justifiably be rethought because the Amendment's authors, back in the Reconstruction era, were focused solely on African Americans and never envisioned the entrance into the United States of millions of undocumented immigrants.

Although it has spread across the country, the phenomenon of illegal immigration is concentrated in the states along the U.S.-Mexico border. It is in these states that the citizenship status of these immigrants' children has been most vocally challenged. In the 1970s, for instance, a Texas school district determined that it did not have to open its doors to the children of illegal immigrants or to those whose citizenship status was unclear. The case ultimately reached the Supreme Court in a case known as *Plyler v. Doe*. There, the Court ruled that no Texas municipality could deny public education to any child living there regardless of that child's citizenship status. Public education, the Court decided, was a general good that balanced out any "unfair" financial or administrative burdens cited by those who opposed providing education to children whose citizenship status was dubious or unclear.

In making its decision in *Plyler v. Doe*, the Court also returned to the basic principles of national versus states' rights that has been at the heart of American history from the Revolutionary era through the Civil War and down to the present day. The state of Texas, the Court concluded, could not limit the rights of people whose American citizenship was guaranteed under the citizenship clause of the Fourteenth Amendment.

# Chronology

**1775–1783**

The American Revolution. Thirteen British colonies along the Atlantic coast of North America successfully break away from Britain to form the United States of America.

**1787**

The Constitutional Convention meets in Philadelphia to begin drafting a constitution by which the United States of America will be governed. The draft is finished by the end of the year.

**1788**

The Constitution is ratified by the required nine of the original thirteen states. The tenth state to ratify is Virginia, which proposes to add to it a Bill of Rights.

**1791**

Congress adds the first ten amendments to the Constitution as the Bill of Rights.

**1857**

The Supreme Court makes its decision in *Scott v. Sandford*, better known as the Dred Scott case. The Court determines that people of African origin, whether slave or free, cannot be citizens of the United States.

**1861–1865**

The American Civil War, fought between the "Confederacy" of eleven breakaway southern states who see their states' rights as being trampled upon by the national government and the "Union" of mostly northern and western states who claim that the Confederacy is unconstitutional. More than 600,000 soldiers die in the conflict.

**1863**

President Abraham Lincoln issues his Emancipation Proclamation, freeing all slaves.

**1865**

The Civil War ends when the Confederate general Robert E. Lee surrenders to his Union counterpart, General Ulysses S. Grant, at the Appomattox, Virginia, Court House on April 9.

**1865**

President Abraham Lincoln is assassinated on April 15. He is replaced as president by Andrew Johnson.

**1865**

In December, following its ratification by the twenty-seventh of the then thirty-six states, the Thirteenth Amendment is added to the U.S. Constitution. It bans all slavery.

**1865–1877**

The Reconstruction era. During this period the United States tries to heal the wounds of the Civil War by reintegrating the Confederate states into the union. Major issues include the status of former slaves and the relationship between the national government and the governments of the states.

**1866**

Congress passes the important Civil Rights Act of 1866 over President Johnson's veto. Targeting African Americans, it gives U.S. citizenship to "all persons born in the United States not subject to any foreign power, excluding Indians not taxed."

**1866**

On June 13 the Fourteenth Amendment is proposed to the U.S. Congress. Connecticut is the first state to ratify it, doing so on June 25. Five other states follow that year, with a total of twenty-eight of the thirty-seven states needed to ratify for the amendment to be added to the Constitution.

**1867**

Fifteen more states ratify the Fourteenth Amendment.

**1868**

A twenty-eighth state, South Carolina, ratifies the Fourteenth Amendment on July 9. Following some uncertainty connected to the removal of ratification in some states and new ratification in others, the Fourteenth Amendment is added to the Constitution on July 28.

**1870**

The Fifteenth Amendment is added to the U.S. Constitution. It prohibits the government from denying voting rights to U.S. citizens based on their racial background, skin color, or previous status of slavery.

**1880–1924**

An era of widespread immigration to the United States. Most of the immigrants come from Europe.

**1882**

Congress passes the Chinese Exclusion Act, seeking to end any further immigration from China and denying citizenship to Chinese immigrants.

**1895**

The Supreme Court issues its decision in *Plessy v. Ferguson*. It allows states to treat people of different racial backgrounds on a "separate but equal" status, thus permitting segregation in schools and other institutions.

**1898**

The Supreme Court decides, in *United States v. Wong Kim Ark*, that a Chinese man born to immigrant parents is a full U.S. citizen because he was born on American soil, a guarantee provided in the Fourteenth Amendment.

## 1907

The "Gentleman's Agreement" between the Japanese and U.S. governments greatly limits any further Japanese immigration to the United States.

## 1924

Congress enacts the 1924 Immigration Act, seeking to limit immigration in general but to encourage relatively more immigration from northern and western Europe.

## 1942

After Japan's attack on the American naval base at Pearl Harbor starts World War II, Japanese immigrants and their children living along the West Coast are forced to move to relocation camps inland. Authorities fear that they may either be the source of anti-American activity or face violent, race-based threats from local populations. The forced moves are very controversial, especially because the second generation of Japanese immigrants, or Nisei, are full citizens by virtue of the Fourteenth Amendment. The government decides, though, that in this instance national security interests outweigh citizenship rights.

## 1958

In the *Perez v. Brownell* decision, the Supreme Court holds that a person can lose his or her American citizenship for reasons including moving to Mexico to avoid military service and voting in a Mexican election.

## 1965

The United States reforms its immigration laws. The new measures, including one based on the principle of "family reunification," open the door to millions of newcomers over the next decades. Thanks to the Fourteenth Amendment's citizenship clause, any children of these newcomers are automatically American citizens.

## 1967

The Supreme Court overturns the *Perez v. Brownell* decision in *Afroyim v. Rusk*. In this decision, the Court determines that Congress does not generally maintain the ability to withdraw American citizenship even if the person concerned voted in a foreign election. The decision helps create precedents by which it is very difficult for an American to lose his or her citizenship, and it also increases the likelihood of people claiming dual citizenship.

## 1982

In *Plyler v. Doe*, the Supreme Court holds that a Texas municipality must provide public education to all children living within its area, even if those children's citizenship status is unclear. The decision creates a precedent by which local governments are required to provide not only education but also other benefits to children of undocumented immigrants.

## 2001

Yasser Hamdi, a U.S. citizen, is captured in Afghanistan while fighting for the Taliban against American-led forces. American officials charge him with being an "illegal enemy combatant," while defenders claim that his rights as an American citizen have been violated because he allegedly has not been granted due process of law. Hamdi is released to Saudi Arabia in 2004 after agreeing to abandon his U.S. citizenship.

## 2007

The Texas congressman and 2008 candidate for president Ron Paul proposes a new constitutional amendment that would overturn the Fourteenth Amendment's citizenship clause.

CONSTITUTIONAL
AMENDMENTS
BEYOND THE BILL OF RIGHTS

CHAPTER 1

# Historical Background on the Fourteenth Amendment

# The Fourteenth Amendment Confirms That African Americans are Indeed U.S. Citizens

*Akhil Reed Amar*

*One of the many steps that led to the outbreak of the American Civil War in 1861 was an 1857 Supreme Court case resulting in what became known as the Dred Scott decision. It proclaimed that people of African origin could never be citizens of the United States, even if they were free from slavery. After the bloody years of the Civil War itself, American leaders tried to enact measures that would repudiate the Dred Scott decision. Among them was the Fourteenth Amendment to the Constitution.*

*In the following selection, Constitutional scholar Akhil Reed Amar examines how the citizenship clause of the Fourteenth Amendment guaranteed the right of citizenship to all people of African origin born on U.S. soil. He also notes that the Amendment removed the ability of any individual state to limit or restrict citizenship rights despite later legal challenges. Akhil Reed Amar is the Southmayd Professor of Law and Political Science at Yale University.*

The Fourteenth Amendment's text began by repudiating the racialist vision of American identity that had animated Chief Justice Taney's infamous *Dred Scott* decision. Taney's 1857 opinion had proclaimed that a black man—even if born free in a state that treated him as a full and equal citizen—could never claim rights of citizenship under the *federal* Constitution. In 1862, [U.S. president Abraham] Lincoln's attorney general opined that free blacks as a rule were federal

Akhil Reed Amar, *America's Constitution: A Biography*, New York: Random House, 2005. Copyright © 2005 by Akhil Reed Amar. All rights reserved. Reproduced by permission of Random House, Inc., in the UK by permission of Writer's Representatives, Inc. on behalf of the author.

citizens, despite Taney's words. The Civil Rights Act of 1866 took aim at *Dred Scott* even more directly by legislating the principle of birthright citizenship: "All persons born in the United States and not subject to any foreign power, excluding Indians not taxed, are hereby declared to be citizens of the United States." Two months later, Congress opened its proposed Fourteenth Amendment with similar anti-Taney language: "All persons born or naturalized in the United States and subject to the jurisdiction thereof, are citizens of the United States and of the State wherein they reside."

The amendment aimed to provide an unimpeachable legal foundation for the earlier statute, making clear that everyone born under the American flag—black or white, rich or poor, male or female, Jew or Gentile—was a free and equal citizen. As with the statute, the amendment did not encompass persons born on American soil who owed allegiance to some other jurisdiction—for instance, children of foreign diplomats or of tribal Indians. The amendment also made clear that non-native, naturalized Americans were entitled to claim the privileges of citizenship. This point could be teased out of other federal statutes and had thus been unnecessary to state in the 1866 Act, but it was worth reiterating in the amendment, lest any negative implication arise in this, the first explicit *constitutional* definition of American citizenship. Perhaps most important, the amendment clarified that to be an American citizen meant having rights not just against the federal government but also against one's home state.

## Defining American Citizenship

These words codified a profound nationalization of American identity. Lacking any explicit definition of American citizenship, the Founders' Constitution [of 1789] was widely read in the antebellum [pre-Civil War] era as making national citizenship derivative of state citizenship, except in cases involving the naturalization of immigrants and the regulation of federal territories. The Fourteenth Amendment made clear that all Americans were in fact citizens of the nation first and foremost, with a status and set of birthrights explicitly affirmed in a national Constitution. Henceforth the nation would not only define national citizenship, but state citizenship as well. Even for persons born on its own soil, a state would no longer enjoy carte blanche to designate some (that is, whites) as "citizens" and to treat others (free blacks) as lesser "inhabitants." Likewise, no state could henceforth bar any American citizen from choosing to become a state citizen—a point only implicit (at best) in the Founders' text. Article IV had obliged South Carolina to treat a Massachusetts *visitor* with a certain respect but had not stated explicitly that a Massachusetts man had an absolute right to *become* a South Carolinian, whatever other South Carolinians might think.

Many first-year law students are told, and today's Supreme Court is fond of reiterating, that the Fourteenth Amendment's key words targeted only the actions of state government. Though this claim may be true of the amendment's second sentence ("No State shall . . ."), it is plainly false as an account of the amendment's first sentence, which entitled citizens to rights against both state and federal officials. In tandem with the amendment's final sentence, these opening words also empowered Congress to dismantle various nongovernmental structures of inequality that threatened the amendment's vision of equal citizenship.

Though the word "equal" did not explicitly appear in the Fourteenth Amendment's first sentence, the concept was strongly implicit. All persons born under the flag were citizens, and thus *equal* citizens. The companion Civil Rights Act had spoken of the right of all citizens to enjoy "full and equal" civil rights, and a later Supreme Court case glossed the citizenship clause as follows: "All citizens are equal before the law." Read alongside Article I's prohibitions on both state and federal titles of nobility, the citizenship clause thus proclaimed an ideal of republican equality binding on state and federal governments alike. Congress, if it chose, could go even further by enforcing the vision of equal citizenship against a host of unequal social structures and institutions. Taney's backdrop *Dred Scott* opinion had located citizenship in a broad context of social meaning and practice above and beyond state action. Blacks, said Taney in notorious language, could not be citizens because they were regarded by the white race—and not merely by white governments—as "beings of an inferior order, and altogether unfit to associate with the white race," with "no rights which the white man is bound to respect."

Thus, when the Fourteenth Amendment overturned Taney, it did so with words suggesting that Congress could use its sweeping *McCulloch*-like enforcement power [based on the 1819 *McCulloch v. Maryland* decision that allowed the federal government to supersede state laws] to enact statutes affirming that blacks were in fact and in law equal citizens worthy of respect and dignity. Such statutes could not compel whites to invite blacks to their dinner parties; such truly private consensual relations lay outside the ambit of equal citizenship. Suffrage rights also lay outside the domain of mere citizenship. For example, white women and children had long been viewed as equal citizens, but this fact did not thereby entitle them to vote. Black citizenship, as conceptualized by the Civil Rights Act and the Civil Rights Amendment, meant full and equal "civil" rights as distinct from "political" rights. But in enforcing the letter and spirit of the citizenship clause, Congress could indeed properly end widespread nongovernmental systems of exclusion in places such as hotels, theaters, trains, and steamships. Congress could also seek to protect blacks from racially motivated violence and thereby make plain that blacks did have rights that white men were bound to respect.

During the Reconstruction era, Congress enacted several statutes to this effect, some of which were struck down by a Supreme Court ill disposed to construe expansively the consti-

*Copy of "Frank Leslie's Illustrated Newspaper" with the front page story on the Supreme Court's anti-abolitionist Dred Scott decision of 1857, including illustrations of the Scott family.*

tutional sentence that had been introduced to chastise the Court itself. The first Justice John Marshall Harlan (not to be confused with his Eisenhower-era grandson) dissented in the most important set of these stingy Reconstruction decisions, the 1883 *Civil Rights Cases* [which banned the federal government from outlawing racial discrimination on the part of individuals], as he would later dissent in *Plessy v. Ferguson* [which permitted racial segregation]. In 1883, Harlan stressed the "distinctly affirmative character" of the citizenship clause and argued that postwar Congresses should have at least as much authority to protect blacks as prewar Congresses had enjoyed to harm them.

## Equality of Citizenship

Thirteen years later, Harlan explained in *Plessy* that the Constitution forbade government from creating a pervasive racial caste system. As Harlan saw it, any law whose preamble explicitly proclaimed blacks to be second-class citizens would plainly violate the Fourteenth Amendment, and the emerging system of racial apartheid known as Jim Crow broadcast precisely this unconstitutional message by its very operation. In purpose, in effect, and in social meaning, Jim Crow stretched its tentacles out to keep blacks down. Its whole point was to privilege whites and degrade blacks, in direct defiance of the Fourteenth Amendment's promise of equal citizenship. Though Jim Crow slyly claimed to provide formal, symmetric equality ("separate but equal"), in reality it delivered substantive inequality that made its regime practically indistinguishable from the postwar Southern Black Codes—the very set of laws that the amendment had undeniably aimed to abolish. Though Justice Harlan saw all this in 1896, his brethren did not. Not until the middle of the twentieth century would Court majorities embrace Harlan's vision, quietly at first and then with increasing confidence and emphasis.

Even as the citizenship clause and the rest of the Fourteenth Amendment plainly took aim at the Black Codes, these words also targeted other—nonracial—forms of discrimination. Whereas the Fifteenth Amendment would later use the language "race, color, or previous condition of servitude" to extend suffrage to black men, the Fourteenth spoke more abstractly of all "citizens" entitled to various "privileges [and] immunities" and of all "persons" with a right to "due process" and "equal protection." At this level of abstraction, the amendment seemed to repudiate a multitude of inequalities beyond Black Codes and race laws.

But how to define this range? From one perspective it might be said that virtually all laws discriminate, treating some persons differently from others. Thus, most criminal codes treat arsonists differently from burglars and both differently from non-felons; tax codes often draw lines between homeowners and renters, between wage earners and dividend recipients, and so on. What makes ordinary tax codes qualitatively different from the Black Codes? Conversely, what sorts of nonracial laws might be more like the Black Codes than the tax codes?

Modern judges have wrestled with these issues by fixing their gaze on the phrase "equal protection" in the Fourteenth Amendment's overworked second sentence. Yet perhaps additional guidance may be found in the overlooked first sentence, and in particular in its key word: "born." The amendment's text summoned up a provocative vision of birthright citizenship: Government could properly regulate its citizens' behavior—their conduct and choices—but should never degrade or penalize a citizen or treat that citizen as globally inferior to others simply because of his or her low birth status. The Black Codes, which subordinated certain people simply because they were born with dark skin, defined the paradigm case of impermissible legislation, but the grand idea that humans were born free and equal opened itself to broader interpretations— some plainly invited by Reconstruction Republicans, others less clearly foreseen yet nonetheless textually permissible. Laws that stigmatized those born out of wedlock, or that discriminated against American-born children of immigrants, or that doled out extra inheritance rights to firstborn children, or that heaped disabilities on anyone born a Jew or born female, or that gave special privileges to scions of the wealthy—all such legislation could plausibly be seen as violative of the equal-birth principle.

## Affirming Equality

The notion that all persons are born/created equal was hardly a new idea in 1866. Lincoln had insisted that this was *the* core idea of the Declaration of Independence, whose main draftsman himself [Thomas Jefferson] had worked to overturn Virginia's primogeniture laws [which gave special rights to firstborn sons] during the Revolution. In a farewell message penned fifty years after the Declaration, Jefferson had also famously reminded his countrymen that "the mass of mankind has not been born with saddles on their backs, nor a favored few booted and spurred, ready to ride them legitimately, by the grace of God." Though the slaveholding Jefferson had not in life practiced what he preached on his deathbed, other Founding-era texts offered sturdier, less ironic foundations upon which Reconstruction Republicans could build. As of 1792, six states had outlawed or moved toward outlawing slavery, and in turn four of these six had enacted a Revolutionary-era state constitution. Every one of these four—and interestingly enough, only these four—featured a clause affirming that "all men" were "born" "equal."

Whereas the Founding text used the word "men" in describing the principle of birthright equality, its Reconstruction descendant did not—and for good reason. Far more than is generally recognized today, the framers of the Reconstruction Amendments focused not merely on the race issue but also on intersecting issues of gender. Urgent questions of status and inequality topped the political agenda in the 1860s in a way that they had not in the 1780s. Once these issues had risen to the surface, conversations about race and sex intertwined in complex and fascinating ways. The justices debating the question of black citizenship in *Dred Scott* had found themselves obliged to ponder female citizenship; the framers of the Thirteenth Amendment had plainly understood that females were half the population seeking emancipation; and . . . women were central political actors in, and subjects of, the great drama surrounding the enactment of the Fourteenth and Fifteenth Amendments.

# The Fourteenth Amendment Emerged Out of an Earlier Civil Rights Act

*Kenneth L. Karst*

*In the following selection, legal scholar Kenneth L. Karst examines how the Thirty-ninth U.S. Congress, which met from 1865 to 1867, tried to enact legislation that might confirm the principles of human equality that the American Civil War, at least in part, had been fought over. The Thirty-ninth Congress is also known as the Reconstruction Congress because it was tasked with the difficult job of rebuilding the American union. Its members faced the challenge of working with one another in the aftermath of a period when the states they represented had been involved in a violent conflict.*

*Karst notes that the Congress passed a Civil Rights Act that sought to guarantee equality of citizenship for all African Americans, including those just freed from slavery. The act survived a presidential veto to become law in April 1866. Since it had faced such pronounced opposition, and since many in Congress were doubtful whether it could be effectively enforced, proponents sought a simpler, broader declaration of citizenship. The Fourteenth Amendment followed. Kenneth L. Karst is a professor of law emeritus at the University of California, Los Angeles.*

A standard feature of war is wartime propaganda. We say we are fighting for an ideal, and we come to believe it. Just as the Revolution had been carried on in the name of liberty and equality, so the Civil War produced volumes of egalitarian rhetoric, much of it taken directly from an antislavery movement that had begun in the eighteenth century. After the

Kenneth L. Karst, *Belonging to America: Equal Citizenship and the Constitution*, New Haven, CT: Yale University Press, 1989. Copyright © 1989 by Yale University. All rights reserved. Reproduced by permission.

war, the major issue before the Reconstruction Congress was the translation of the ideal of equality into institutions that would govern human affairs. Not many in that Congress, it appears, really believed that blacks and whites should be treated as social equals. It was a legal equality that they sought to achieve through the adoption of civil rights laws and constitutional amendments.

## The Quest for Redemption

The wartime Emancipation Proclamation and the immediate postwar ratification of the Thirteenth Amendment had already begun the nation's quest for redemption for the sin of slavery. But constitutional abolition was not enough. The Thirteenth Amendment took effect in December 1865. By mid-March eight southern states had adopted their versions of the Black Codes—laws systematically imposing legal disabilities on blacks. The codes were designed to exclude blacks from real membership in southern society and to keep them in a status of inferiority and dependence closely resembling slavery. The laws forbade blacks to own or transfer property, to inherit, to purchase, or to seek access to the courts. By combining vagrancy laws with a convict-lease system, they even assured that the former slaves would continue to serve as laborers for the planters. To abolish this new variation on the old theme of racial caste, Congress adopted the Civil Rights Act of 1866.

The first section of the Act provided:

*[A]ll persons born in the United States* and not subject to any foreign power, excluding Indians not taxed, *are hereby declared to be citizens of the United States: and such citizens*, of every race and color [including former slaves], *shall have the same right*, in every State and territory of the United States, to make and enforce contracts, to sue, be parties, and give evidence, to inherit, purchase, lease, sell, hold, and convey

*A close-up of a draft of Article XIV, or the Fourteenth Amendment to the U.S. Constitution, which outlines the rights and privileges of citizenship.* Hulton Archive/Getty Images.

real and personal property, and to full and equal benefit of all laws and proceedings for the security of person and property, *as is enjoyed by white citizens*, and shall be subject

43

to like punishment, pains, and penalties, and to none other, any statute, ordinance, regulation, or custom, to the contrary notwithstanding.

As the emphasized words make clear, these civil rights were written into the law as the equal rights of citizens; the *Dred Scott* decision [which in 1857, denied citizenship to people of African origin] was repudiated. The act plainly proceeds on the assumption that certain substantive rights are necessary if the newly declared citizenship for the freed slaves is to be more than a hollow form. Black and white citizens are to have equal benefit of both laws and proceedings—the practical business of enforcement of rights—for securing their persons and property. Not only judges but sheriffs and tax collectors and governmental officers generally are to respect that equality of status by affording black people equal treatment. Access to the courts is guaranteed on an equal basis, too; a black person is to have his or her say in court—to be heard out, treated as a person and not an object, as any other respected citizen would be heard. Blacks are to be afforded participation in the governmental process as parties and as witnesses. More generally, they are offered participation in the community's public life: buying and selling, dealing with property, protecting their rights—all on the same terms as white citizens.

## Citizenship Caries Both Rights and Responsibilities

Respect and participation, yes—but responsibility, too. To be a citizen is not merely to be a consumer of rights, but to stand with other citizens in a relation of mutual responsibilities. Indeed, the recognition (by law and otherwise) of members' responsibilities to one another is one of the chief indicators that a community exists. Under the act, black citizens are to be held to their contracts, their leases, their deeds; as for misdeeds, they are to be subject to the same punishments as are white citizens. Most importantly, through working and acquiring property they are to have a real chance to take responsibility for their own and their families' well-being. In fulfilling this responsibility they can provide for their families by making wills, and their spouses and children can inherit—all in their capacities as citizens.

In short, the 1866 Civil Rights Act recognized that the goal of equal citizenship—respected and responsible participation in the public life of the society—could not be achieved through a bare declaration of citizenship as a formal status, but needed substantive underpinnings. Equality and belonging were melded into a single policy, as was entirely natural, given the framers' objectives. President Andrew Johnson had similarly linked the ideas of citizenship and equality in his message vetoing the bill. Congress overrode the veto, and the act became law on April 9, 1866, one year to the day after [Confederate commander Robert E.] Lee's surrender at Appomattox [ending the Civil War].

The proponents of the 1866 act initially assumed that Congress had the power to enact it under the Thirteenth Amendment. Johnson's veto message, however, challenged this assumption about congressional power. The proposed Fourteenth Amendment had been under consideration for two months before the veto; at least from this time forward, one of the chief objectives of the amendment's framers was to secure the 1866 act from constitutional attack. Whether or not one accepts [legal scholar and civil rights activist] Jacobus tenBroek's argument that the equal protection clause was intended as a substantive guarantee of full protection of fundamental or natural rights, it is beyond dispute that the focus of congressional discussion of the proposed Fourteenth Amendment was the eradication of racial discrimination in the enjoyment of the rights of citizens spelled out in the 1866 act.

The full text of the Fourteenth Amendment's first section occupies only two sentences. The first one says:

> All persons born or naturalized in the United States, and subject to the jurisdiction thereof, are citizens of the United States and of the State where they reside.

Plainly, this provision aims at constitutionalizing the rejection of the *Dred Scott* opinion by making clear that citizenship does not depend on race. The second sentence sets out three statements of rights:

> No State shall make or enforce any law which shall abridge the privileges or immunities of citizens of the United States; nor shall any State deprive any person of life, liberty, or property, without due process of law; nor deny to any person within its jurisdiction the equal protection of the laws.

The text of the amendment's first section thus bears one striking similarity to the 1866 act, and one striking difference. The amendment follows the pattern of the act in declaring citizenship and then setting out a series of rights that can readily be understood as rights of citizens. But where the act proceeds from a declaration of citizenship to a detailed listing of specific rights of citizens, the amendment's three prohibitory clauses are couched in grand generalities, words obviously capable of bearing larger meanings.

## Broad, Vague Language

The privileges and immunities clause was added to the proposed amendment late in the drafting process. Although it is scarcely a model of crisp definition, the clause does, of course, guarantee something to citizens. In the hands of a receptive judiciary it would have been an apt vessel for a constitutional protection of the citizenship rights set out in the 1866 act. But the congressional debates show that even if this clause had not been added, the framers expected the amendment to serve the purpose of guaranteeing the equal rights of citizens. There was no serious effort to differentiate the functions of the various clauses—privileges and immunities, due process, equal protection—of section 1 of the amendment. With or without the privileges and immunities clause, the section in its entirety was taken to guarantee equality in the enjoyment of the rights of citizenship.

[Constitutional law scholar] Charles L. Black, Jr., has argued that even if all three of the prohibitions of section 1 had been omitted, most of what has been done in their names might have been accomplished on the basis of the section's first sentence. Black's argument of chief concern to us is that the conferral of citizenship empowers Congress, in enforcing the Fourteenth Amendment, to forbid racial discrimination both public and private. But he also draws from this same sentence in section 1 a wide range of rights of citizens, including those due process rights that the Supreme Court has found to be the essentials of a "scheme of ordered liberty."

The declaration of citizenship was added by the drafters of the Fourteenth Amendment "almost as an afterthought." It was not part of the amendment as the House of Representatives first adopted it but was inserted at the last minute in the Senate, with minimal discussion. In the absence of legislative history, we are left to speculate on the framers' purposes in adding the sentence. [Constitutional scholar] Alexander Bickel advanced two possible explanations. First, the senators might have thought it provident to make clear who was a citizen of the United States, given that the privileges and immunities clause seemed to attach significance to that status. Second, by providing "a definition of citizenship in which race played no part," the framers ensured that "*Dred Scott* was effectively, which is to say constitutionally, overruled." Surely Bickel was right, yet the two purposes he suggested do not exhaust all the possible reasons for adding this definition of citizenship to the proposed amendment. For one thing, the addition of the sentence heightens the textual parallel of the amendment to the first section of the 1866 act, thus strengthening the conclusion that the clauses that follow the definition of citizenship are designed to protect the substantive rights of citizens. Second, the overruling of *Dred Scott* is consistent not only with the narrow purpose to confer the legal status of citizenship on persons born in this country but also with a broader purpose to abolish the system of caste recognized in that opinion, by giving a particular substantive content to the amendment.

# It Is Absurd to Consider Former Slaves Anything Other than Full Citizens

*James F. Wilson*

*In his Emancipation Proclamation of 1863, President Abraham Lincoln declared that the institution of slavery was ended in the United States and that all former slaves were now free people. But it took until 1865, when Lincoln's Union armies defeated their Southern Confederate counterparts, to ensure that the proclamation would truly take effect. Even then there was much debate over the true status of former slaves, with the Democratic Party of the time hesitant to grant them full citizenship.*

*In the following selection, Senator James F. Wilson argues that former slaves must be considered full citizens. He cites a number of earlier legal and scholarly opinions to assert that they must not only be considered citizens but that the federal government, and not the individual states, has the right to ensure their status. Wilson's argument was made during congressional debates over an 1866 Civil Rights Act, the prelude to the Fourteenth Amendment.*

It is in vain we look into the Constitution of the United States for a definition of the term "citizen." It speaks of citizens, but in no express terms defines what it means by it. We must depend on the general law relating to subjects and citizens recognized by all nations for a definition, and that must lead us to the conclusion that every person born in the United States is a natural-born citizen of such States, except it may be that children born on our soil to temporary sojourners or representatives of foreign Governments, are native-born citizens of the United States. Thus it is expressed by a writer on the Constitution of the United States:

James F. Wilson, "Rights of Citizens," *The Congressional Globe*, March 1, 1866, p. 1117.

"Every person born within the United States, its Territories, or districts, whether the parents are citizens or aliens, is a natural-born citizen in the sense of the Constitution, and entitled to all the rights and privileges appertaining to that capacity." —*Rawle on the Constitution.*

And this writer continues, as if he intended a refutation of the position assumed by some persons at this time, that a negro is neither a citizen nor an alien, but a mere person with no definable national character, and adds:

"It is an error to suppose, as some have done, that a child is born a citizen of no country, and subject of no Government, and that he so continues till the age of discretion, when he is at liberty to put himself under what Government he pleases."

## An Indefensible Position

No nation, I believe, ever did recognize this absurd doctrine; and the only force it ever had in this country, was that given it by the Democratic party which used the negro as a football for partisan games. The growing importance of the colored race in the United States, now that the entire race is free, will soon cause even the Democratic party to abandon the indefensible position it occupies on this question. That we have six million persons in this Government subject to its laws, and liable to perform all the duties and support all the obligations of citizens, and yet who are neither citizens nor aliens, is an absurdity which cannot survive long in the light of these days of progressive civilization.

It will not be denied by any one, I presume, that the English doctrine which claims as a subject every person born within the jurisdiction of the Crown, made negroes born in the colonies out of which the original thirteen States were created, British subjects; nor will it be contended that they were not citizens of the States after the States threw off their allegiance to the mother country, and being citizens of the States that they became, on the establishment of the Government of the United States, citizens of the United States. A very clear statement of this doctrine occurs in the case of the State *vs.* Manuel, 3 Devereaux & Battle's N.C.R., page 26, in these words:

> "The term 'citizen' as understood in our law is purely analogous to the term subject in the common law, and the change of phrase has entirely resulted from the change of government. The sovereignty has been transferred from one man to the collective body of the people, and he who before was a 'subject of the king is now a citizen of the State.'"

This position is maintained by Rawle on the Constitution, page 80; Kent's Commentaries, volume two, lecture twenty-five; Lawrence's Appendix to Wheaton on International Law. I might multiply authorities, but I have referred to enough for my purpose. By our law colored persons are citizens of the United States. Of this there can be no reasonable doubt; and we have been too tenaciously devoted to the doctrine "once a citizen always a citizen" to strike out of our column of citizens six million persons in obedience to any such political irrationality as lies buried in the Dred Scott case.

But, sir, suppose I should admit for the sake of an argument that negroes are not citizens, would that be an objection to the power of Congress to enact the provision of this bill to which I have called the attention of the House? If they are not citizens may we not naturalize them? If this can be done, then in either view of the case the provision of the bill which I am now discussing is proper, and is not obnoxious to the objection that we do not possess the power to pass it.

## Bestowing Citizenship

The Constitution, in article one, section eight, provides that Congress shall have power "to establish a uniform rule of naturalization." This does not mean that the power of Congress exhausts itself by being once used, nor that there can be but one rule, nor that the rule established must provide that the naturalization shall be by action upon single or individual cases, nor yet that only foreigners can be thus made citizens. The practice of the Government is against all these positions. The rule must be uniform in its operation upon the class affected by it, and must not be confined in terms in its operation to any particular State or district of country, except when it operates only on a particular class of persons who may be occupying a limited district of country. Several statutes, establishing as many different rules, each uniform in itself, have been enacted on this subject. Most of these rules provide for the naturalization by individual cases:

> "But a collective naturalization may also take place, of a class of persons, natives of the country or otherwise, and who, without any act on the part of the individuals, may be made citizens."—*Lawrence's Appendix to Wheaton on International Law; Opinion of Attorney General Cushing, in Opinions of Attorneys General.*

The power thus to naturalize collectively has been exercised in several instances by the Government. The most striking case is that which is found in the act of March 3, 1843, in which it is provided that the

> "Stockbridge tribe of Indians, and each and every of them, shall be deemed to be, and from that time declared to be, citizens of the United States."

Mr. Speaker, these authorities are sufficient upon this point, and I will leave the question of citizenship as presented in the first part of this section, and call the attention of the House to the next proposition of the section as proposed to be amended by the committee. It is in these words:

> There shall be no discrimination in civil rights or immunities among citizens of the United States in any State or Ter-

ritory of the United States on account of race, color, or previous condition of slavery; and such citizens of every race and color, without regard to any previous condition of slavery or involuntary servitude, except as a punishment for crime whereof the party shall have been duly convicted, shall have the same right to make and enforce contracts, to sue, be parties and give evidence, to inherit, purchase, lease, sell, hold, and convey real and personal property, and to full and equal benefit of all laws and proceedings for the security of person and property as is enjoyed by the white citizens, and shall be subject to like punishment, pains, and penalties, and to none other, any law, statute, ordinance, regulation, or custom, to the contrary notwithstanding.

This part of the bill will probably excite more opposition and elicit more discussion than any other; and yet to my mind it seems perfectly defensible. It provides for the equality of citizens of the United States in the enjoyment of "civil rights and immunities." What do these terms mean? Do they mean that in all things civil, social, political, all citizens, without distinction of race or color, shall be equal? By no means can they be so construed. Do they mean that all citizens shall vote in the several States? No; for suffrage is a political right which has been left under the control of the several States, subject to the action of Congress only when it becomes necessary to enforce the guarantee of a republican form of government. Nor do they mean that all citizens shall sit on the juries, or that their children shall attend the same schools. These are not civil rights or immunities. Well, what is the meaning? What are civil rights? I understand civil rights to be simply the absolute rights of individuals, such as—

"The right of personal security, the right of personal liberty, and the right to acquire and enjoy property." "Right itself, in civil society, is that which any man is entitled to have, or to do, or to require from others, within the limits of prescribed law." —Kent's Commentaries.

To use the language of Attorney General Bates, in the opinion already cited, "The word rights is generic, common, embracing whatever may be lawfully claimed." The definition given to the term "civil rights" in Bouvier's Law Dictionary is very concise, and is supported by the best authority. It is this:

> "Civil rights are those which have no relation to the establishment, support, or management of government."

From this it is easy to gather an understanding that civil rights are the natural rights of man; and these are the rights which this bill proposes to protect every citizen in the enjoyment of throughout the entire dominion of the Republic.

# The Fourteenth Amendment Would Establish Federal Despotism over the Individual States

*A.J. Rogers*

*One of the major causes of the Civil War was a different under-standing of the proper relationship between the federal govern-ment of the United States and the individual states. Many South-ern states, most notably, did not believe that the federal government had the right, under the Constitution, to enact laws that would be binding on all states. Instead, their representatives and leaders argued, the Southern states had the right to main-tain the institution of slavery if they so desired, and the national government had no right to say otherwise. The debate over this relationship remained heated in the Reconstruction era that fol-lowed the Civil War.*

*In the following selection, Representative A.J. Rogers of New Jersey argues before his colleagues in the House of Representa-tives in 1866 that the proposed Fourteenth Amendment denies individual states the right to enact their own laws with regard to freed slaves. This denial, he asserts, amounts to the establishment of federal tyranny over the states. He is especially concerned with the granting of full citizenship rights, in every state, to all Afri-can Americans. This, he fears, might lead to increases in mixed marriage, mixed education, and other manifestations of "equal-ity" between black people and white people. Throughout Rogers argues that such matters should be left to the individual states.*

Who gave the Senate the constitutional power to pass that bill guarantying equal rights to all, if it is necessary to amend the organic law in the manner proposed by this joint

A.J. Rogers, "Rights of Citizens," in *The Appendix to the Congressional Globe*, Febru-ary 26, 1866, pp. 134–135.

resolution [the Fourteenth Amendment]? This is but another attempt to consolidate the power of the States in the Federal Government. It is another step to an imperial despotism. It is but another attempt to blot out from that flag the eleven stars that represent the States of the South and to consolidate in the Federal Government, by the action of Congress, all the powers claimed by the Czar of Russia or the Emperor of the French. It provides that all persons in the several States shall have equal protection in the right of life, liberty, and property. Now, it is claimed by gentlemen upon the other side of the House that negroes are citizens of the United States. Suppose that in the State of New Jersey negroes are citizens, as they are claimed to be by the other side of the House, and they change their residence to the State of South Carolina, if this amendment be passed Congress can pass under it a law compelling South Carolina to grant to negroes every right accorded to white people there; and as white men there have the right to marry white women, negroes, under this amendment, would be entitled to the same right; and thus miscegenation and mixture of the races could be authorized in any State, as all citizens under this amendment are entitled to the same privileges and immunities, and the same protection in life, liberty, and property.

## Privileges and Immunities

Will gentlemen upon the other side dispute my position? I defy contradiction. Why, sir, it says that the people of each State shall have the privileges and immunities of citizens in the several States. What is a privilege? What an immunity? Will learned gentlemen deny that the right of marriage is a contract and a privilege. Its source is the law of nature, whence it has flowed into the municipal laws of every civilized country, and into the general law of nations. The organic law says that no person but a natural-born citizen, or a citizen when it was made, shall be eligible to the office of President. This amendment would make all citizens eligible, negroes as well as whites. For if negroes are citizens, they are natural born, because they are the descendants of ancestors for several generations back, who were born here as well as themselves. The negroes cannot be citizens in a new State in which they may take up their residence unless they are entitled to the privileges and immunities of the citizens resident in that State. Most of the States make a distinction in the rights of married women. This would authorize Congress to repeal all such distinctions.

Marriage is a contract as set down in all the books from the Year-books down to the present time. A white citizen of any State may marry a white woman; but if a black citizen goes into the same State he is entitled to the same privileges and immunities that white citizen have, and therefore under this amendment a negro might be allowed to marry a white woman. I will not go for an amendment of the Constitution to give a power so dangerous, so likely to degrade the white men and women of this country, which would put it in the power of fanaticism in times of excitement and civil war to allow the people of any State to mingle and mix themselves by marriage with negroes so as to run the pure white blood of the Anglo-Saxon people of the country into the black blood of the negro or the copper blood of the Indian.

Now, Sir, the words "privileges and immunities" in the Constitution of the United States have been construed by the courts of the several States to mean privileges and immunities in a limited extent. It was so expressly decided in Massachusetts by Chief Justice [Isaac] Parker, one of the ablest judges who ever sat upon the bench in the United States. Those words, as now contained in the Constitution of the United States, were used in a qualified sense, and subject to the local control, dominion, and the sovereignty of the States. But this act of Congress proposes to amend the Constitution so as to take away the rights of the States with regard to the life, liberty, and property of the people, so as to enable and empower Congress to pass laws compelling the abrogation of all the statutes of the States which makes a distinction, for instance, between a crime committed by a white man and a crime committed by a black man, or allow white people privileges, immunities, or property not allowed to a black man.

## Different States, Different Rights

Take the State of Kentucky, for instance. According to her laws, if a negro commits a rape upon a white woman he is punished by death. If a white man commits that offense, the punishment is imprisonment. Now, according to this proposed amendment, the Congress of the United States is to have the right to repeal the law of Kentucky and compel that State to inflict the same punishment upon a white man for rape as upon a black man.

According to the organic law of Indiana a negro is forbidden to come there and hold property. This amendment would abrogate and blot out forever that law, which is valuable in the estimation of the sovereign people of Indiana.

In the State of Pennsylvania there are laws which make a distinction with regard to the schooling of white children and the schooling of black children. It is provided that certain schools shall be designated and set apart for white children, and certain other schools designated and set apart for black children. Under this amendment, Congress would have power to compel the State to provide for white children and black children to attend the same school, upon the principle that all the people in the several States shall have equal protection in all the rights of life, liberty, and property, and all the privileges and immunities of citizens in the several States.

The effect of this proposed amendment is to take away the power of the States; to interfere with the internal police and regulations of the States; to centralize a consolidated power in this Federal Government which our fathers never intended should be exercised by it. All men who are honest, and love their country, and who believe in the doctrines upon which the constitutional liberty of this country is founded, must admit that the rights of the States were the most jealous rights which our fathers had in view; and when they wrested from England the independence of the several States, they wrested them as thirteen independent States and nations, free from each other, with all rights and privileges given to the people to exercise, carry into effect, and control a Government according to their own exclusive will and judgment.

# Reconstruction Inspired Political Debate and Public Violence

*Eric Foner*

*In the following selection, historian Eric Foner describes the heated political atmosphere of the Reconstruction era that followed the Civil War. "Radical" Republicans pursued governmental reforms based on equality and civil rights, while more cautious figures, such as President Andrew Johnson, wanted to move more slowly. Johnson, for his part, had taken office only upon the assassination of Abraham Lincoln in April 1865.*

*As Foner notes, Johnson's hesitancy and arrogance inspired ever bolder steps on the part of the Radical Republicans, among them the proposal of the Fourteenth Amendment. During the congressional elections of 1866, these and other controversies spilled over into political violence. The Radicals gained control of Congress and were thus able to enact the Fourteenth Amendment despite President Johnson's opposition. Indeed, for many alleged offenses, Johnson found himself the target of impeachment proceedings in both 1867 and 1869, although both attempts failed to remove him from office. Eric Foner is Dewitt Clinton Professor of History at Columbia University and the author of many books on the Reconstruction era and other topics.*

When Congress assembled in December 1865, [President Andrew] Johnson announced that Reconstruction effectively was over. Governments led by men loyal to the Union had been established in the South, he declared, and all Congress had to do to complete "the work of restoration" was to seat their elected representatives. In response, Radicals ["Radi-

Eric Foner, *Forever Free: The Story of Emancipation and Reconstruction*, New York: Alfred A. Knopf, 2005. Copyright © 2005 by Forever Free, Inc. All rights reserved. Used by permission of Alfred A. Knopf, a division of Random House, Inc.

cal" Republicans] such as [Thaddeus] Stevens and [Charles] Sumner called for the abrogation of the Johnson governments and the establishment of new ones based on equality before the law and male suffrage. The more numerous moderates, however, still hoped to work with Johnson, and these proposals got nowhere. Nonetheless, the moderates were not prepared to embrace the president's Reconstruction plan without modifications. Congress refused to seat the representatives and senators elected from the southern states, many of whom had been leading officials in the Confederate government and army. It established a Joint Committee on Reconstruction, and set about debating the proper course of action.

Much of the ensuing discussion revolved around the problem, as [Senator Lyman] Trumbull put it, of defining "what slavery is and what liberty is." "We must see to it," announced Senator William Stewart of Nevada, "that the man made free by the Constitution of the United States is a freeman indeed." To the Radicals, freedom was "a right so universal," in the words of another congressman, that it must apply to all Americans and no longer be limited by race. Moderate Republicans believed that further federal measures were necessary to protect blacks' civil rights. "Their present nominal freedom is nothing but a mockery," wrote Illinois Republican leader Jesse Fell shortly after Congress assembled. Equality before the law, enforced if necessary by national authority, had become the moderates' requirement for restoring the South to full participation in the Union.

Two bills reported to the Senate soon after the New Year by Lyman Trumbull, chairman of the Senate Judiciary Committee, embodied the moderates' policy of leaving Johnson's governments in place but adding federal protection of the freedpeople's rights. The first bill extended the life of the Freedmen's Bureau [a federal organization that aided freed slaves], scheduled to expire within a few months. The second, the Civil Rights Bill, was a far more important measure that for the first time offered a legislative definition of American citizenship. The bill declared all persons born in the United States (except Indians) national citizens, and went on to spell out the rights they were to enjoy equally without regard to race. Equality before the law was central to the measure—no longer could states enact laws such as the Black Codes declaring certain actions crimes for black persons but not white. So too were free-labor values: no state could deprive any citizen of the right to make contracts, bring lawsuits, or enjoy equal protection of the security of person and property. Although the bill addressed primarily discrimination by state officials, it also contained the intriguing word *custom*, suggesting that private acts also fell within its purview. No state law or custom could deprive any citizen of what Trumbull called the "fundamental rights belonging to every man as a free man." The bill allowed federal marshals and district attorneys to bring suit against violations—with cases to be heard in federal, not state, courts—and allowed aggrieved individuals to sue for civil damages.

## The Meaning of Freedom

In constitutional terms, the Civil Rights Bill represented the first attempt to give concrete meaning to the Thirteenth Amendment, which ended slavery, to define in legislative terms the essence of freedom. If states could deny blacks the rights specified in the measure, asked one congressman, "then I demand to know, of what practical value is the amendment abolishing slavery?" The bill said nothing of the right to vote. Nonetheless, it reflected how profoundly the Civil War had altered traditional federal-state relations and weakened traditional racism. A mere nine years earlier, the U.S. Supreme Court, in the Dred Scott decision, had decreed that no black person could be a citizen of the United States. Before the war, Congressman James G. Blaine later wrote, only "the wildest fancy of a distempered brain" could have envisioned a law of

Congress according blacks "all the civil rights pertaining to a white man." Although clearly directed against the South, the bill had a national scope, and it invalidated many discriminatory laws in the North as well. "I admit that this species of legislation is absolutely revolutionary," declared Senator Lot M. Morrill of Maine. "But are we not in the midst of a revolution?"

Although most of his cabinet urged him to approve these measures, Johnson vetoed both the Freedmen's Bureau and Civil Rights bills. He insisted that Congress pass no Reconstruction legislation until the southern states were fully represented—a position, as one senator correctly predicted, that meant that "he will and must . . . veto every other bill we pass." In the Freedmen's Bureau Bill veto, Johnson claimed that he, not Congress, represented the will of the people. "This is modest," one Republican remarked, "for a man made president by an assassin."

Johnson's vetoes deployed arguments opposing federal action on behalf of African Americans that have been repeated ever since, including in our own time, by critics of civil rights legislation and affirmative action. He appealed to fiscal conservatism, raised the specter of an immense federal bureaucracy trampling on citizens' rights, and insisted that self-help, not dependence on government handouts, was the surest path to individual advancement. Congress, he insisted, had neither the need nor the authority to protect the freedpeople's rights. Assistance by the Freedman's Bureau would encourage blacks to believe that they did not have to work for a living, thereby encouraging them to lead a "life of indolence." Johnson called the civil rights measure a "stride toward centralization of all legislative powers in the national Government." Although he did not use the modern term "reverse discrimination," the president somehow persuaded himself that by acting to secure the rights of blacks, Congress would be discriminating against white Americans—"the distinction of race and color is by the bill made to operate in favor of the colored and against the white race."

Johnson also delivered an intemperate speech to a crowd at the White House in February 1866 condemning the Radicals and hinting that they were responsible for Lincoln's assassination. Singling out Stevens, Sumner, and abolitionist Wendell Phillips by name, he asked, "does not the murder of Lincoln appease the vengeance and the wrath of the opponents of this government?" But more significant than Johnson's intemperate language, his vetoes ended all chance of cooperation with Congress. Although the Senate failed by a single vote to override the Freedmen's Bureau Bill veto (another measure, enacted in July, extended the bureau's life to 1870), Congress mustered the two-thirds majority to pass the Civil Rights Act. For the first time in American history, a significant piece of legislation became law over a president's veto.

## Presidential Stubbornness

Johnson's intransigence also impelled Republicans to devise their own plan of Reconstruction, and to write their understanding of the consequences of the Civil War into the Constitution, there to be secure from shifting electoral majorities. The result was the Fourteenth Amendment, approved by Congress in 1866 and ratified two years later. It enshrined for the first time in the Constitution the ideas of birthright citizenship and equal rights for all Americans. The amendment, Stevens told the House, gave a constitutional foundation to the principle that state laws "shall operate *equally* upon all." "I can hardly believe," he added, "that any person can be found who will not admit that . . . [it] is just." Unlike the Civil Rights Act, which listed specific rights all citizens were to enjoy, the Fourteenth Amendment used far more general language. It prohibited states from abridging any citizen's "privileges and immunities" or denying them "due process" or the "equal protection of the law." This broad language opened the door for future Congresses and the federal courts to breathe meaning into the guarantee of legal equality, a process that occupied the courts for much of the twentieth century. The amendment also struck a blow against the Johnson governments in the South by prohibiting leading Confederate officials from holding office unless granted amnesty by Congress.

None of the measures of 1866 accorded black men the right to vote. The Fourteenth Amendment finessed that issue by leaving suffrage qualifications to be determined by the states but providing that if a state deprived any group of men of the franchise, it would lose some of its representatives in Congress. (The penalty did not apply, however, if the state denied women the right to vote.) The Fourteenth Amendment was a moderate measure, not a creation of the Radicals. Rather than forging a "perfect republic" from the ruins of slavery by purging American institutions of "inequality of rights," Stevens told the House on the eve of its passage, "I find we shall be obliged to be content with patching up the worst portions of the ancient edifice, and leaving it, in many of its parts, to be swept through by the storms of despotism." Nonetheless, Stevens said, he would vote for passage. Why? "Because I live among men and not among angels."

Stevens realized that whatever their limitations, the Civil Rights Act and the Fourteenth Amendment embodied a profound change in the federal system and the nature of American citizenship. The abolitionist doctrine of equal citizenship as a birthright had now been written into the Constitution. The principle of equality before the law, moreover, did not apply only to the South or to blacks. Like the Civil Rights Act, the Fourteenth Amendment invalidated many northern laws that discriminated on the basis of race. And, as one congressman noted, it affected the rights of "the millions of people of foreign birth who will flock to our shores."

## Political Violence

With the passage of the Fourteenth Amendment, the Republican majority in Congress prepared to do battle with the president. Already thoroughly alienated from the Republican Party, Johnson found his position further weakened by incidents of violence in the South. In May, an altercation that began when two horse-drawn hacks, one driven by a white man, the other by a black, collided on a Memphis street, escalated into three days of racial violence. White mobs, aided and abetted by the city police, assaulted blacks on the streets and invaded their neighborhoods. By the time order had been restored, at least forty-eight persons, nearly all of them black, had been killed and hundreds of dwellings, schools, and churches looted or destroyed.

Three months later, another violent outbreak took place in New Orleans. Governor James M. Wells, a Johnson appointee, had become more and more alarmed at ex-Confederate control of the Louisiana legislature and local government in New Orleans. He decided to reconvene the Constitutional Convention of 1864, which had recessed but never adjourned, in order to press for black suffrage. On July 20, 1866, when the gathering was set to assemble, a white mob led by local police descended on a march of several hundred black supporters of the convention. In the melee that followed, some thirty-eight persons were killed and 146 wounded, mostly blacks. After investigating the affair, General Philip H. Sheridan called it "an absolute massacre." The New Orleans riot did more than any other single event to arouse northern public opinion against the president. The role of the city police in contributing to the violence rather than restoring order suggested that the southern governments of Presidential Reconstruction were unwilling or unable to protect the basic rights of citizens.

The events of 1866 also roused white southern Unionists to political action. Some broke with their region's racial heritage to support black suffrage. A small minority in most states, whites who had supported the Union cause during the war were numerous enough in areas such as the hill country of North Carolina, Georgia, Tennessee, and Arkansas to have hoped that Reconstruction would place them in power. Johnson's policies had dealt a severe blow to this ambition. During 1866, more and more southern Unionists gravitated to the congressional side in the Reconstruction debate. They pressed for Congress to bar leading Confederates from power, sometimes urging the wholesale disenfranchisement of "rebels." Some, reluctantly, began to embrace the idea of black suffrage, if only to oust ex-Confederates from power. William G. Brownlow—the "fighting parson" of the East Tennessee mountains who had been elected as the state's governor in 1865 after Johnson, then military governor, had barred supporters of the Confederacy from the polls—said "one more law" was needed to complete Reconstruction, "a law enfranchising the negroes . . . to weigh down the balance against rebeldom." The growing outspokenness of southern Unionists helped to persuade Congress that the possibility existed of creating a biracial Republican Party in the South.

## A Tense Presidential Election

The Fourteenth Amendment became the central issue in the Congressional elections of 1866. In the fall, the president broke with tradition by embarking on a speaking trip across the North, the "swing around the circle," intended to drum up support for candidates who supported his Reconstruction policies and opposed ratification of the Fourteenth Amendment. The tour was a political disaster. Johnson could not refrain from responding in kind to hecklers and launching tirades against his congressional opponents. On one occasion, he intimated that divine intervention had removed Lincoln and elevated *him*, Johnson, to the White House. In St. Louis, he compared himself to Jesus Christ, with Thaddeus Stevens as his Judas. The spectacle further destroyed his credibility and contributed to a sweeping Republican victory in the fall elections. But the main cause of the outcome was popular disaffection from Presidential Reconstruction and the widespread conviction that further steps had to be taken to protect the rights of the former slaves and place the South under the control of men genuinely "loyal" to the Union. Despite the results, however, and egged on by Johnson and the northern Democratic press, all the southern states except Tennessee refused to ratify the Fourteenth Amendment.

Once again, the intransigence of Johnson and the white South played into the Radicals' hands. When Congress reassembled in December 1866, Republicans set out to fashion a completely new plan of Reconstruction. They ignored Johnson. The president, declared the *New York Herald*, previously his supporter, "forgets that we have passed through the fiery ordeal of a mighty revolution, and that the pre-existing order of things is gone and can return no more." Numerous proposals circulated in Congress—reducing the southern states to territories, disenfranchising former Confederates, confiscating property, impeaching the president.

After much debate, Republicans coalesced around a new Reconstruction Act, passed over Johnson's veto early in March 1867. The act rested on the premise that lawful governments did not exist in the South, and that Congress could govern the region until acceptable ones had been established. It turned the political clock back to "the point where [Union general Ulysses S.] Grant left off the work, at Appomattox Court House [where the Civil War ended]," declared one member of Congress. The Reconstruction Act temporarily divided the South into five military districts and outlined how new governments, based on male suffrage (with the exception of leading Confederate officials, who could not vote in forthcoming elections), would be established. The southern states must ratify the Fourteenth Amendment and adopt new constitutions embodying the principle of manhood suffrage without regard to race. Interracial democracy, the dream of abolition-ists, Radical Republicans, and the former slaves, had finally come to the South. Thus began the period of Radical, or con-gressional, Reconstruction, which lasted until the fall of the last southern Republican governments in 1877.

The laws and amendments of Reconstruction reflected the intersection of two products of the Civil War era—a newly empowered national state and the idea of a national citizenry enjoying equality before the law. Rather than a threat to lib-erty, the federal government, declared Charles Sumner, had become "the custodian of freedom." What Republican leader Carl Schurz called "the great Constitutional revolution" of Re-construction transformed the federal system, and with it, the language of rights so central to American political culture. Be-fore the Civil War, disenfranchised groups were far more likely to draw inspiration from the Declaration of Independence than the Constitution. (The only mention of equality in the original Constitution, after all, had occurred in the clause granting each state an equal number of senators.) But the re-writing of the Constitution during Reconstruction suggested that the rights of individual citizens were intimately connected to federal power.

# The Fourteenth Amendment Will Help America Fulfill Its Promise

*Thaddeus Stevens*

*Thaddeus Stevens (1792–1868), whose speech before Congress in March 1868 makes up the following selection, was one of the most powerful members of Congress during the Civil War and Reconstruction years. A representative of Pennsylvania, Stevens rose to become one of the so-called Radical Republicans who advocated a strong military effort in the defense of the American Union from 1861 to 1865 as well as the strong turn toward federal enforcement of civil rights during Reconstruction. He was one of the chief voices in favor of the citizenship clause of the Fourteenth Amendment.*

*In his speech, Stevens argues that the Fourteenth Amendment will fulfill the promise of legal equality contained in the Declaration of Independence of 1776. His particular focus is on that most basic of democratic rights, the right to vote, and on the fact that the Fourteenth Amendment prevents any individual state from restricting or limiting that right.*

Before the Constitution was amended I could not agree with some of my learned friends that Congress could intermeddle with State laws relative to the elective franchise in the United States. The circumstance of slavery seemed, while it was submitted to, to prevent it. After the amendment abolishing slavery I still doubted, and proposed a constitutional remedy on the 5th of December, 1865, in the following words:

> "All national laws shall be equally applicable to every citizen, and no discrimination shall be made on account of race and color."

Thaddeus Stevens, *The Selected Papers of Thaddeus Stevens: Volume 2, April 1865– August 1868*, Pittsburgh: University of Pittsburgh Press, 1998. Copyright © 1998, University of Pittsburgh Press. All rights reserved. Reproduced by permission.

Since the adoption of the fourteenth amendment, however, I have no doubt of our full power to regulate the elective franchise, so far as it regards the whole nation, in every State of the Union, which, when tried, I hope, will be so formed as to be beneficial to the nation, just to every citizen, and carry out the great designs of the framers of the Government, according to their views expressed in the Declaration of Independence.

It cannot fail to be beneficial and convenient, when we consider the trouble and inconvenience which a citizen of one State encounters when he travels temporarily into another. Instead of being a brother at home he is now an alien in his native land. While he participates in all the burdens and anxieties of Government, he is forbidden, if a non-resident, to take part in selecting the magistrate who is to rule his destinies for the next four years.

In this there is no principle of republican justice. The Constitution of 1789 did not carry out the principles of government which were intended by the fathers when in 1776 they laid the foundations of the Government on which this nation was built. Then they had been inspired with such a light from on high as never man was inspired with before in the great work of providing freedom for the human race through a government in which no oppression could find a resting-place.

They contemplated the erection of a vast empire over the whole continent which in its national character should be governed by laws of a supreme, unvarying character. While municipal institutions with self-control might be granted for convenience, it was never intended that one half of this nation should be governed by one set of laws and the other half by another and conflicting set on the same subject.

The laws, the principle, which were to apply to the dwellers on the Penobscot [River] were to apply as those on the Savannah and Susquehanna [rivers]; else the Declaration would have proclaimed that the one—the people on the Penobscot or Susquehanna—were born free and equal, and those on the Savannah with a modified equality; that the one had inalienable rights, among which was liberty; that the other had inalienable rights, but perfect liberty was not among them. The grand idea of those immortal men was that there were certain rights, privileges, and immunities which belonged to every being who had an immortal soul, none of which should be taken from him, nor could he surrender them in any arrangement with society.

## Rights Cannot Be Taken Away

So essential to the repose of the whole community was it that every man should possess each of these rights, privileges, and immunities, that he was forbidden by his Creator to part with them. He could not sell himself, he could not sell his children, into slavery. He could not sell his life for a price. He could not surrender the right to pursue his own happiness. Every attempt to do so was nugatory. Every instrument founded upon such a contract, no matter how solemn, no matter how hedged about by broad seals, no matter how stamped by State legislation and executive approval, none of these things gave it life. It was null and void; it was a corpse incapable of animation.

I am speaking now of the original design of the framers of the Declaration of Independence, who had determined that there were certain principles which, to give perfect liberty, should apply alike to every human being. Who can deny this position without laying a heavier burden upon one human being than another without being authorized to do so by their common Creator? Who can doubt that if you put such power into the hands of the best men it will be abused, unless restrained by equal laws? Why should one man be more responsible to his temporal or eternal governor than another and be punished by different rules? I know that when they came to frame the Constitution, slavery having increased, they were

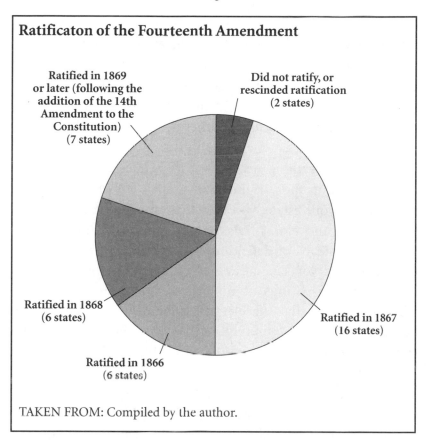

## Ratificaton of the Fourteenth Amendment

Ratified in 1869 or later (following the addition of the 14th Amendment to the Constitution) (7 states)

Did not ratify, or rescinded ratification (2 states)

Ratified in 1868 (6 states)

Ratified in 1867 (16 states)

Ratified in 1866 (6 states)

TAKEN FROM: Compiled by the author.

obliged to postpone some of those universal principles, and allow individuals and municipalities to violate them for awhile. I thank God that necessity no longer exists. The law-givers of America are now as free to act as [the biblical figure] Sampson [usually spelled Samson] when the fire had touched the flax. May they never again be beguiled by any conservative Delilah [the woman who betrayed Samson] to suffer their locks to be shorn and their limbs to be bound by the withes [branches] of a twisted Constitution.

The laws which were then intended to be universal must now be made universal. The principles which were intended to govern the whole American nationality must now be made to cover and control the whole national action throughout this grand empire. Towns, corporations, and municipalities may be allowed their separate organizations not inconsistent therewith, but must not incorporate any principles in conflict with those great rights, privileges, and immunities. What are those rights, privileges, and immunities? Without excluding others, three are specifically enumerated—life, liberty, and the pursuit of happiness. These are universal and inalienable. It follows that everything necessary for their establishment and defense is within those rights. You grant a lot or easement in the midst of your estate; you thereby grant the right of way to it by ingress and egress. Disarm a community and you rob them of the means of defending life. Take away their weapons of defense and you take away the inalienable right of defending liberty. This brings us now directly to the argument by which we prove that the elective franchise is a right of the Declaration and not merely a privilege, and is one of the rights and immunities pronounced by that instrument to be "inalienable."

If, as our fathers declared, "all just government is derived from the assent of the governed;" if in federal republics that assent can be ascertained and established only through the ballot, it follows that to take away that means of communication is to take away from the citizen his great weapon of defense and reduce him to helpless bondage. It deprives him of an inalienable right. This clearly proves that the elective franchise ranks with "life" and "liberty" in its sacred, inalienable character. But, while the Declaration clearly proves what the intention then was, the action of the Convention in framing the Constitution of the United States, it seemed to me, bartered away for the time being some of those inalienable rights, and, instigated by the hellish institution of slavery, suspended one of the muniments of liberty. Having thus shown that the elective franchise is one of the inalienable rights of man, without which his liberty cannot be defended, and that it was suspended by the arbitrary Constitution of 1789, let us see if that suspension has been removed, so as to leave our hands unrestrained in restoring its full vigor while still acting under the Constitution. That right appertains to every citizen. But while this suspension existed the natural love of despotism induced communities to hold that each State might fix the qualifications, rights, and deprivations of its own citizens.

The fourteenth amendment, now so happily adopted, settles the whole question and places every American citizen on a perfect equality so far as merely national rights and questions are concerned. It declares that—

> "All persons born or naturalized in the United States and subject to the jurisdiction thereof are citizens of the United States and of the State wherein they reside. No State shall make or enforce any law which shall abridge the privileges and immunities of citizens of the United States, nor shall any person be deprived of life, liberty, or property, without due process of law; nor deny any person within its jurisdic tion the equal protection of the laws."

# America Committed Itself to Citizenship for People of All Ethnicities

*Earl Warren*

*In 1968 the New York University School of Law held a confer-
ence to commemorate the 100-year anniversary of the passage of
the Fourteenth Amendment. Among the participants was Earl
Warren, chief justice of the U.S. Supreme Court from 1953 to
1969. The following selection is from a talk that Warren gave at
the conference.*

*Warren, who supported much of the civil rights legislation
enacted in the 1950s and 1960s, notes that the Fourteenth
Amendment provided a guarantee of full legal equality for all
U.S. citizens. Notably, it guaranteed citizenship for African
Americans born in the United States. He also states that, despite
the promise of the Fourteenth Amendment and the other two
Reconstruction Amendments, full, real equality had yet to be
achieved. Warren spoke in the context of the late 1960s, when, in
an atmosphere of race-based insecurity and violence, a presidential commission found that African Americans and other non-
whites still faced discrimination.*

To a scientist contemplating our ageless universe, a century
can be as fleeting as a falling star streaking to a flaming
death in the earth's atmosphere. But to ordinary mortals contemplating their own mortality, 100 years impart a permanence and stability to an institution or—in our case—a document. Particularly in today's rapidly changing world, endurance
for 100 years is a marvelous achievement, and one worthy of
celebration. However, endurance for 100 years provides not

Earl Warren, *The Fourteenth Amendment: Centennial Volume*, New York: New York
University Press, 1970. Copyright © 1970 by New York University. All rights reserved.
Reproduced by permission.

only proof of survival but also a needed perspective for an evaluation of progress made or opportunities lost, and it is in this latter respect that a centennial observance can be a sobering experience. For we find in such observances an opportunity to pause and to take stock—to determine if the promises and hopes of a century past have come to fruition—and to put the lessons of the past 100 years to work in plotting a course for the next century.

The Fourteenth Amendment is sorely in need of such a sobering evaluation. That amendment—along with the Thirteenth and Fifteenth Amendments—wrote into our basic charter of government a solemn commitment by the American people to the goal of equality before the law. By that commitment, the American people pledged through their government that no opportunity would be denied an individual because of his race or his color or his country of origin.

Yet, as we stand here today, 100 years after that solemn commitment was undertaken, we would be less than honest with ourselves if we did not admit that only now do we as a nation stand on the threshold of translating that promise of equality into realistic action.

I do not mean to imply that the past century has been without its achievements. Only the most cynical among us would contend that the Negro—the intended beneficiary of the solemn commitment of the Fourteenth Amendment—is no better off today than he was in those tragic days immediately following the Civil War. But the steps we have taken in the last 100 years toward fulfilling the promise of equality have been halting and uncertain. We have learned in recent years—and at a cost which this nation cannot long bear—that promises and piecemeal progress are no substitute for true equality. We have seen that the rising aspirations of Negro Americans and their just desire for meaningful participation in American life will no longer be stilled by the promise of a better tomorrow. We have seen further that we can no longer counsel patience when men are denied the employment they seek, when their children are denied a quality education, and when their families are denied adequate housing and the food necessary to sustain life simply because their skins are black. And we have received dire warnings that, unless we quickly put our national house in order, the fires fanned by racism will ultimately consume the entire structure. No thoughtful American can long ignore the tragic implications of the warning issued by the Presidential Commission which studied the causes of recent riots in our major cities. "This is our conclusion," the commission wrote. "Our Nation is moving toward two societies, one black, one white—separate and unequal." . . .

## A Promise Unfulfilled

I make no pretense of having easy solutions to the many problems which plague our nation today and which touch upon the principles of democracy embodied in the Fourteenth Amendment. Merely to catalogue those problems and the correlative principles in the amendment would be too ambitious an undertaking on this occasion. I propose a more limited inquiry. I shall examine what I view as the core commitment of the Fourteenth Amendment—the pledge to the newly freed slaves that henceforth they would enjoy equality with their former masters—and what I perceive as the reasons that the commitment has so long remained a promise unfulfilled. In particular, I shall focus on the respective roles played by Congress and the Supreme Court in enforcing the Fourteenth Amendment during the past century.

Such an examination will necessarily dwell upon the failings of the past, and the tone of my remarks may occasionally sound negative and harsh in their criticisms. By the emphasis I have chosen, I do not mean to denigrate the achievements of the past century. Indeed, without those achievements, I could not say with confidence that I believe we stand at the threshold of making the Fourteenth Amendment's promise of equal-

*Issues surrounding citizenship and equal rights were topics of public discussion and debate, as depicted in this illustration from the late 1800s.* ©Bettmann/Corbis.

ity a reality. But the past century has also been marked by a number of failings and misdirections, and unless we fully understand the nature of those failings, we may find that our next century of experience with the Fourteenth Amendment will be one of delusion rather than progress.

# From Slavery to Freedom

The roots of American democracy are firmly embedded in the doctrine of equality. When Thomas Jefferson took his pen in hand to write the Declaration of Independence, he listed as the first of the "self-evident" truths "that all men are created equal." Those were strong words for that age, but they were hardly novel or original. As Professor Robert Harris has observed, the Declaration of Independence succinctly and eloquently summarized the major elements of Western democratic thought which gave birth to the American Revolution. Equality was a consistent theme in the works of those men who made the major contributions to Western political theory up to the time of the Revolution. The writings of [English philosopher] John Locke were particularly influential among the men who led the American Revolution, and the concept of the equality of men was an important part of Locke's theories of the social compact and natural law. It was to be expected that Lockean concepts of equality should find expression in the words of the men who fought to establish this nation.

The progress of the nation toward its stated goal of equality is, however, a story filled with ironies. Thus, the author of the ringing words of the Declaration of Independence was a slaveholder, and some of his writings suggest that he viewed the Negro as anything but the white man's equal. And, while the document which heralded the birth of the nation spoke of the equality of all men, the constitution which welded the former colonies into a single government relegated the Negroes imported from Africa as slaves to a second-class status. Yet, ultimately, it was the slavery compromise of 1787 which made possible and necessary the commitment to equality now embodied in the three Civil War amendments. For, while the slavery compromise forced an abandonment of the concept of equality, it was a compromise held together by the mortar of convenience and expediency.

As sectional differences developed and grew in the new nation, the compromise began to crumble, and the institution of slavery came to symbolize the bitter divisions in the country. As new compromises were attempted to preserve that most inhumane of human institutions, the fight against slavery assumed the posture of a moral crusade in the North and parts of the West. The Abolitionists, as had Thomas Jefferson before them, drew upon the theories of John Locke in formulating their legal and moral arguments against slavery. But moral pleas fell on deaf ears, and appeals to the fundamental creed of equality contained in the Declaration of Independence were of no avail. Sectional cleavages widened; the South clung stubbornly to the institution of slavery; and the nation was plunged into a tragic civil war when the efforts to preserve the Union by peaceful means failed.

The work of reconstructing the divided and battlescarred nation after the Civil War took many forms. Most relevant for our purposes were the successful efforts to write into our charter of government a constitutional basis for the nation's commitment to the concept of equality. Within five years after the guns of the Civil War had been silenced, Congress had proposed and the country had ratified three amendments which purported to give the newly freed slaves civil and political equality with all other Americans. The Thirteenth Amendment told the Negro that slavery could have no place in this nation and that he could no longer be treated as chattel, to be bought and sold at the caprice of his white master. The Fourteenth Amendment conferred national citizenship on the Negro and told him that he could expect due process and equal protection before the law. The Fifteenth Amendment gave the Negro the most potent weapon in the democratic arsenal— the vote—and promised him that he could participate fully in the American political process. The three amendments had a common feature—they designated the Congress as the governmental body that would take action to ensure that the new commitment to equality would be fulfilled.

# CHAPTER 2

# Testing the Fourteenth Amendment's Citizenship Clause

# The Fourteenth Amendment Ensures Citizenship to All People Born on U.S. Soil

*Horace Gray*

*In 1882 the United States enacted its first-ever measure to limit immigration. Known as the Chinese Exclusion Act, it was designed to end any further immigration from China as well as deny citizenship to such newcomers. Thousands of Chinese people had already come to the United States, mostly to California, where they were first drawn by the 1849 Gold Rush and then by jobs helping to build railroads. But by the 1880s both the gold fields and available work were thinning. Arguing that the Chinese could simply not assimilate in the United States because of the vast cultural differences between them and Western European immigrant groups, the Chinese Exclusion Act's proponents succeeded in closing off Chinese immigration altogether until new laws were passed in the twentieth century.*

*The following selection is from a Supreme Court decision made in 1898, which was one of the first decisions to elaborate on the Fourteenth Amendment's citizenship clause. The case concerned a young man named Wong Kim Ark, whose parents were Chinese immigrants but who was born in California. Upon returning to San Francisco in 1895 from a visit to China, Wong had been denied permission to enter the country on the grounds that he was not a U.S. citizen. When the case reached the Supreme Court, the majority opinion, delivered here by Justice Horace Gray, was that Wong was indeed an American citizen by virtue of the Fourteenth Amendment's guarantees. Congress, Justice Gray noted, did not have the ability to remove the citizenship of a naturalized American whose citizenship rights were made clear by the Constitution. Therefore in Wong's case the*

Horace Gray, "*U.S. v. Wong Kim Ark*," in U.S. Supreme Court, 169 U.S. 649 (1898), March 28, 1898.

*Chinese Exclusion Act could not apply. It might apply to Wong's immigrant parents, but because he had been born on U.S. soil, Wong himself was an American citizen.*

Sol. Gen. Conrad, for the United States.

Thomas D. Riordan, Maxwell Evarts, and J. Hubley Ashton, for appellee.

Mr. Justice GRAY, after stating the facts in the foregoing language, delivered the opinion of the court.

The facts of this case, as agreed by the parties, are as follows: Wong Kim Ark was born in 1873, in the city of San Francisco, in the state of California and United States of America, and was and is a laborer. His father and mother were persons of Chinese descent, and subjects of the emperor of China. They were at the time of his birth domiciled residents of the United States, having previously established and are still enjoying a permanent domicile and residence therein at San Francisco. They continued to reside and remain in the United States until 1890, when they departed for China; and, during all the time of their residence in the United States, they were engaged in business, and were never employed in any diplomatic or official capacity under the emperor of China. Wong Kim Ark, ever since his birth, has had but one residence, to wit, in California, within the United States and has there resided, claiming to be a citizen of the United States, and has never lost or changed that residence, or gained or acquired another residence and neither he, nor his parents acting for him, ever renounced his allegiance to the United States, or did or committed any act or thing to exclude him therefrom. In 1890 (when he must have been about 17 years of age) he departed for China, on a temporary visit, and with the intention of returning to the United States, and did return thereto by sea in the same year, and was permitted by the collector of customs to enter the United States, upon the sole ground that he was a native-born citizen of the United States. After such return, he remained in the United States, claiming to be a citizen thereof, until 1894, when he (being about 21 years of age, but whether a little above or a little under that age does not appear) again departed for China on a temporary visit, and with the intention of returning to the United States; and he did return thereto, by sea, in August, 1895, and applied to the collector of customs for permission to land, and was denied such permission, upon the sole ground that he was not a citizen of the United States.

It is conceded that, if he is a citizen of the United States, the acts of congress known as the 'Chinese Exclusion Acts,' prohibiting persons of the Chinese race, and especially Chinese laborers, from coming into the United States, do not and cannot apply to him.

The question presented by the record is whether a child born in the United States, of parents of Chinese descent, who at the time of his birth are subjects of the emperor of China, but have a permanent domicile and residence in the United States, and are there carrying on business, and are not employed in any diplomatic or official capacity under the emperor of China, becomes at the time of his birth a citizen of the United States, by virtue of the first clause of the fourteenth amendment of the constitution: 'All persons born or naturalized in the United States, and subject to the jurisdiction thereof, are citizens of the United States and of the state wherein they reside.' . . .

## Expanding the Meaning of Citizenship

The constitution of the United States, as originally adopted, uses the words 'citizen of the United States' and 'natural-born citizen of the United States.' By the original constitution, every representative in congress is required to have been 'seven years a citizen of the United States,' and every senator to have been 'nine years a citizen of the United States'; and 'no person except a natural-born citizen, or a citizen of the United States at the time of the adoption of this constitution, shall be eligible to the office of president.' The fourteenth article of amendment, besides declaring that 'all persons born or naturalized in the United States, and subject to the jurisdiction thereof, are citizens of the United States and of the state wherein they reside,' also declares that 'no state shall make or enforce any law which shall abridge the privileges or immunities of citizens of the United States; nor shall any state deprive any person of life, liberty, or property, without due process of law; nor deny to any person within its jurisdiction the equal protection of the laws.' And the fifteenth article of amendment declares that 'the right of citizens of the United States to vote shall not be denied or abridged by the United States, or by any state, on account of race, color, or previous condition of servitude.'

The constitution nowhere defines the meaning of these words, either by way of inclusion or of exclusion, except in so far as this is done by the affirmative declaration that 'all persons born or naturalized in the United States, and subject to the jurisdiction thereof, are citizens of the United States.' . . .

## Citizenship Cannot Be Based on National Origin

It thus clearly appears that, during the half century intervening between 1802 and 1855, there was no legislation whatever for the citizenship of children born abroad, during that period, of American parents who had not become citizens of the United States before the act of 1802; and that the act of 1855, like every other act of congress upon the subject, has, by express proviso, restricted the right of citizenship, thereby conferred upon foreign-born children of American citizens, to those children themselves, unless they became residents of the United States. Here is nothing to countenance the theory that a general rule of citizenship by blood or descent has displaced in this country the fundamental rule of citizenship by birth within its sovereignty.

So far as we are informed, there is no authority, legislative, executive, or judicial, in England or America, which maintains or intimates that the statutes (whether considered as declaratory, or as merely prospective) conferring citizenship on foreign-born children of citizens have superseded or restricted, in any respect, the established rule of citizenship by birth within the dominion. Even those authorities in this country which have gone the furthest towards holding such statutes to be but declaratory of the common law have distinctly recognized and emphatically asserted the citizenship of native-born children of foreign parents.

Passing by questions once earnestly controverted, but finally put at rest by the fourteenth amendment of the constitution, it is beyond doubt that, before the enactment of the civil rights act of 1866 or the adoption of the constitutional amendment, all white persons, at least, born within the sovereignty of the United States, whether children of citizens or of foreigners, excepting only children of ambassadors or public ministers of a foreign government, were native-born citizens of the United States.

In the forefront, both of the fourteenth amendment of the constitution, and of the civil rights act of 1866, the fundamental principle of citizenship by birth within the dominion was reaffirmed in the most explicit and comprehensive terms.

The civil rights act, passed at the first session of the Thirty-Ninth congress [1865–1867], began by enacting that 'all persons born in the United States, and not subject to any foreign power, excluding Indians not taxed, are hereby declared to be citizens of the United States; and such citizens, of every race and color, without regard to any previous condition of slavery or involuntary servitude, except as a punishment for crime whereof the party shall have been duly convicted, shall have the same right, in every state and territory in the United States, to make and enforce contracts, to sue, be parties and give evidence, to inherit, purchase, lease, sell, hold and convey real and personal property, and to full and equal benefit of all laws and proceedings for the security of person and property, as is enjoyed by white citizens, and shall be subject to like punishment, pains and penalties, and to none other, any law, statute, ordinance, regulation or custom, to the contrary notwithstanding.'

The same congress, shortly afterwards, evidently thinking it unwise, and perhaps unsafe, to leave so important a declaration of rights to depend upon an ordinary act of legislation, which might be repealed by any subsequent congress, framed the fourteenth amendment of the constitution, and on June 16, 1866, by joint resolution, proposed it to the legislatures of the several states; and on July 28, 1868, the secretary of state issued a proclamation showing it to have been ratified by the legislatures of the requisite number of states.

The first section of the fourteenth amendment of the constitution begins with the words, 'All persons born or naturalized in the United States, and subject to the jurisdiction thereof, are citizens of the United States and of the state wherein they reside.' As appears upon the face of the amendment, as well as from the history of the times, this was not intended to impose any new restrictions upon citizenship, or to prevent any persons from becoming citizens by the fact of birth within the United States, who would thereby have become citizens according to the law existing before its adoption. It is declaratory in form, and enabling and extending in effect. Its main purpose doubtless was, as has been often recognized by this court, to establish the citizenship of free negroes. . . . But the opening words, 'All persons born,' are general, not to say universal, restricted only by place and jurisdiction, and not by color or race . . .

To hold that the fourteenth amendment of the constitution excludes from citizenship the children born in the United States of citizens or subjects of other countries, would be to deny citizenship to thousands of persons of English, Scotch, Irish, German, or other European parentage, who have always been considered and treated as citizens of the United States. . . .

## Citizenship Origins Defined

The fourteenth amendment of the constitution, in the declaration that 'all persons born or naturalized in the United States, and subject to the jurisdiction thereof, are citizens of the United States and of the state wherein they reside,' contemplates two sources of citizenship, and two only, birth and naturalization. Citizenship by naturalization can only be acquired by naturalization under the authority and in the forms of law. But citizenship by birth is established by the mere fact of birth under the circumstances defined in the constitution. Every person born in the United States, and subject to the jurisdiction thereof, becomes at once a citizen of the United States, and needs no naturalization. A person born out of the jurisdiction of the United States can only become a citizen by being naturalized, either by treaty, as in the case of the annexation of foreign territory, or by authority of congress, exercised either by declaring certain classes of persons to be citizens, as in the enactments conferring citizenship upon foreign-born children of citizens, or by enabling foreigners individually to become citizens by proceedings in the judicial tribunals, as in the ordinary provisions of the naturalization acts.

The power of naturalization, vested in congress by the constitution, is a power to confer citizenship, not a power to take it away. 'A naturalized citizen,' said Chief Justice Marshall, 'becomes a member of the society, possessing all the rights of a native citizen, and standing, in the view of the constitution, on the footing of a native. The constitution does not authorize congress to enlarge or abridge those rights. The simple power of the national legislature is to prescribe a uniform rule of naturalization, and the exercise of this power exhausts it, so far as respects the individual. The constitution then takes him up, and, among other rights, extends to him the capacity of suing in the courts of the United States, precisely under the same circumstances under which a native might sue.' Congress having no power to abridge the rights conferred by the constitution upon those who have become naturalized citizens by virtue of acts of congress, a fortiori [with even stronger reason] no act or omission of congress, as to providing for the naturalization of parents or children of a particular race, can affect citizenship acquired as a birthright, by virtue of the constitution itself, without any aid of legislation. The fourteenth amendment, while it leaves the power, where it was before, in congress, to regulate naturalization, has conferred no authority upon congress to restrict the effect of birth, declared by the constitution to constitute a sufficient and complete right to citizenship.

No one doubts that the amendment, as soon as it was promulgated, applied to persons of African descent born in the United States, wherever the birthplace of their parents might have been; and yet, for two years afterwards, there was no statute authorizing persons of that race to be naturalized. If the omission or the refusal of congress to permit certain classes of persons to be made citizens by naturalization could be allowed the effect of correspondingly restricting the classes of persons who should become citizens by birth, it would be in the power of congress, at any time, by striking negroes out of the naturalization laws, and limiting those laws, as they were formerly limited, to white persons only, to defeat the main purpose of the constitutional amendment.

The fact, therefore, that acts of congress or treaties have not permitted Chinese persons born out of this country to become citizens by naturalization, cannot exclude Chinese persons born in this country from the operation of the broad and clear words of the constitution: 'All persons born in the United States, and subject to the jurisdiction thereof, are citizens of the United States.'

# The Fourteenth Amendment's Citizenship Clause Is Contrary to Legal Tradition and Sets a Dangerous Precedent

*Melville Fuller*

*The following selection is taken from U.S. Supreme Court justice Melville Fuller's dissenting opinion in the* United States v. Wong Kim Ark *case decided in 1898. In it, Justice Fuller takes issue with the Court's majority opinion that Wong Kim Ark, born in the United States but of Chinese descent, is a fully naturalized U.S. citizen according to the rights guaranteed in the Fourteenth Amendment.*

*Fuller notes that Wong's parents were not themselves U.S. citizens, since they were immigrants to this country who had not been naturalized and could not now be naturalized because of the 1882 Chinese Exclusion Act. He also claims that throughout the legal history of both the United States and even Great Britain (upon which American law is largely based), courts and governments have decided that citizenship is based on one's parentage rather than one's place of birth, implying that the Fourteenth Amendment's citizenship clause should not be as broadly applied as the Court's majority would have it. For Fuller, Chinese immigrants were too "alien," and perhaps bound too much by their allegiance to their own emperor, to be full American citizens. In this he cites an 1892 Supreme Court case,* Fong Yue Ting v. United States, *which focused on the "alien" nature of Chinese people and placed certain restrictions on the movements of some of them.*

Melville Fuller, "*U.S. v. Wong Kim Ark*," in U.S. Supreme Court, 169 U.S. 649 (1898), March 28, 1898.

M<sup>r.</sup> Chief Justice FULLER, with whom concurred Mr. Justice HARLAN, dissenting.

I cannot concur in the opinion and judgment of the court in this case.

The proposition is that a child born in this country of parents who were not citizens of the United States, and under the laws of their own country and of the United States could not become such—as was the fact from the beginning of the government in respect of the class of aliens to which the parents in this instance belonged—is, from the moment of his birth, a citizen of the United States, by virtue of the first clause of the fourteenth amendment, any act of congress to the contrary notwithstanding.

The argument is that although the constitution prior to that amendment nowhere attempted to define the words 'citizens of the United States' and 'natural-born citizen,' as used therein, yet that it must be interpreted in the light of the English common-law rule which made the place of birth the criterion of nationality; that that rule 'was in force in all the English colonies upon this continent down to the time of the Declaration of Independence, and in the United States afterwards, and continued to prevail under the constitution as originally established'; and 'that, before the enactment of the civil rights act of 1866 and the adoption of the constitutional amendment, all white persons, at least, born within the sovereignty of the United States, whether children of citizens or of foreigners, excepting only children of ambassadors or public ministers of a foreign government, were native-born citizens of the United States.'

Thus, the fourteenth amendment is held to be merely declaratory, except that it brings all persons, irrespective of color, within the scope of the alleged rule, and puts that rule beyond the control of the legislative power.

If the conclusion of the majority opinion is correct, then the children of citizens of the United States, who have been

*Supreme Court Chief Justice Melville Weston Fuller. Fuller served from 1890 to 1910.* © Corbis.

born abroad since July 28, 1868, when the amendment was declared ratified, were and are aliens, unless they have or shall, on attaining majority, become citizens by naturalization in the United States; and no statutory provision to the contrary is of any force or effect. And children who are aliens by descent, but born on our soil, are exempted from the exercise of the power to exclude or to expel aliens, or any class of aliens, so often maintained by this court, an exemption apparently disregarded by the acts in respect of the exclusion of persons of Chinese descent. . . .

## The Role of Chinese Heritage

Generally speaking, I understand the subjects of the emperor of China—that ancient empire, with its history of thousands of years, and its unbroken continuity in belief, traditions, and government, in spite of revolutions and changes of dynasty—to be bound to him by every conception of duty and by every principle of their religion, of which filial piety is the first and greatest commandment; and formerly, perhaps still, their penal laws denounced the severest penalties on those who renounced their country and allegiance, and their abettors, and, in effect, held the relatives at home of Chinese in foreign lands as hostages for their loyalty. And, whatever concession may have been made by treaty in the direction of admitting the right of expatriation in some sense, they seem in the United States to have remained pilgrims and sojourners as all their fathers were. At all events, they have never been allowed by our laws to acquire our nationality, and, except in sporadic instances, do not appear ever to have desired to do so.

The fourteenth amendment was not designed to accord citizenship to persons so situated, and to cut off the legislative power from dealing with the subject. . . .

But the Chinese, under their form of government, the treaties and statutes, cannot become citizens nor acquire a permanent home here, no matter what the length of their stay may be.

In *Fong Yue Ting v. United States* [a case dealing with the rights of Chinese immigrants], it was said, in respect of the treaty of 1868 [the Burlingame Treaty, which authorized further Chinese immigration]: 'After some years' experience under that treaty, the government of the United States was brought to the opinion that the presence within our territory of large numbers of Chinese laborers, of a distinct race and religion, remaining strangers in the land, residing apart by themselves, tenaciously adhering to the customs and usages of their own country, unfamiliar with our institutions, and apparently incapable of assimilating with our people, might endanger good order, and be injurious to the public interests; and therefore requested and obtained from China a modification of the treaty.'

It is not to be admitted that the children of persons so situated become citizens by the accident of birth. On the contrary, I am of opinion that the president and senate by treaty, and the congress by legislation, have the power, notwithstanding the fourteenth amendment, to prescribe that all persons of a particular race, or their children, cannot become citizens, and that it results that the consent to allow such persons to come into and reside within our geographical limits does not carry with it the imposition of citizenship upon children born to them while in this country under such consent, in spite of treaty and statute.

In other words, the fourteenth amendment does not exclude from citizenship by birth children born in the United States of parents permanently located therein, and who might themselves become citizens; nor, on the other hand, does it arbitrarily make citizens of children born in the United States of parents who, according to the will of their native government and of this government, are and must remain aliens.

Tested by this rule, Wong Kim Ark never became and is not a citizen of the United States, and the order of the district court should be reversed.

# A Naturalized U.S. Citizen Cannot Have His or Her Citizenship Taken Away Without Consent

*Hugo Black*

*In 1950 Beys Afroyim, a Polish immigrant who had become a naturalized U.S. citizen, moved to Israel. There he voted in a presidential election. When he tried to renew his American passport in 1960, he was refused on the grounds that, by having voted in a foreign election, he forfeited his U.S. citizenship. He sued the U.S. government, naming Secretary of State Dean Rusk as the defendant. When the Supreme Court took up the case, it decided that Afroyim, as a naturalized U.S. citizen, could not have his citizenship rights removed without his consent. The decision was a close one, with five of nine justices supporting the majority opinion.*

*Justice Hugo Black, who delivered the majority opinion in Afroyim's favor, claimed that the Fourteenth Amendment superseded any power that Congress might claim to remove a person's citizenship. He noted that even though the Fourteenth Amendment was originally intended to protect the citizenship of African Americans, legal precedents had demonstrated that it applied to all citizens, whether born on U.S. soil or naturalized. Indeed, the Fourteenth Amendment ensures that Congresses, which by their nature are only temporary, cannot restrict a citizen's permanent rights. In delivering its decision, the Court overruled an earlier one, Perez v. Brownell (1958), which claimed that Congress had the right to withdraw citizenship based on acts the potential expatriate had performed voluntarily, such as voting in a foreign election as Afroyim had.*

Hugo Black, "*Afroyim v. Rusk,*" in U.S. Supreme Court, 387 U.S. 253 (1967), May 1967.

M R. JUSTICE BLACK delivered the opinion of the Court.

Petitioner, born in Poland in 1893, immigrated to this country in 1912 and became a naturalized American citizen in 1926. He went to Israel in 1950, and in 1951 he voluntarily voted in an election for the Israeli Knesset, the legislative body of Israel. In 1960, when he applied for renewal of his United States passport, the Department of State refused to grant it on the sole ground that he had lost his American citizenship by virtue of 401(c) of the Nationality Act of 1940, which provides that a United States citizen shall "lose" his citizenship if he votes "in a political election in a foreign state." Petitioner then brought this declaratory judgment action in federal district court alleging that 401(e) violates both the Due Process Clause of the Fifth Amendment and 1, cl. 1, of the Fourteenth Amendment, which grants American citizenship to persons like petitioner. Because neither the Fourteenth Amendment nor any other provision of the Constitution expressly grants Congress the power to take away that citizenship once it has been acquired, petitioner contended that the only way he could lose his citizenship was by his own voluntary renunciation of it. Since the Government took the position that 401(e) empowers it to terminate citizenship without the citizen's voluntary renunciation, petitioner argued that this section is prohibited by the Constitution. The District Court and the Court of Appeals, rejecting this argument, held that Congress has constitutional authority forcibly to take away citizenship for voting in a foreign country based on its implied power to regulate foreign affairs. Consequently, petitioner was held to have lost his American citizenship regardless of his intention not to give it up. This is precisely what this Court held in *Perez v. Brownell*. . . .

The fundamental issue before this Court here, as it was in *Perez*, is whether Congress can consistently with the Fourteenth Amendment enact a law stripping an American of his citizenship which he has never voluntarily renounced or given up. The majority in *Perez* held that Congress could do this because withdrawal of citizenship is "reasonably calculated to effect the end that is within the power of Congress to achieve." That conclusion was reached by this chain of reasoning: Congress has an implied power to deal with foreign affairs as an indispensable attribute of sovereignty; this implied power, plus the Necessary and Proper Clause, empowers Congress to regulate voting by American citizens in foreign elections; involuntary expatriation is within the "ample scope" of "appropriate modes" Congress can adopt to effectuate its general regulatory power. Then, upon summarily concluding that "there is nothing in the . . . Fourteenth Amendment to warrant drawing from it a restriction upon the power otherwise possessed by Congress to withdraw citizenship" the majority specifically rejected the "notion that the power of Congress to terminate citizenship depends upon the citizen's assent."

## Congress Cannot Rescind Citizenship

First we reject the idea expressed in *Perez* that, aside from the Fourteenth Amendment, Congress has any general power, express or implied, to take away an American citizen's citizenship without his assent. This power cannot, as *Perez* indicated, be sustained as an implied attribute of sovereignty possessed by all nations. Other nations are governed by their own constitutions, if any, and we can draw no support from theirs. In our country the people are sovereign and the Government cannot sever its relationship to the people by taking away their citizenship. Our Constitution governs us and we must never forget that our Constitution limits the Government to those powers specifically granted or those that are necessary and proper to carry out the specifically granted ones. The Constitution, of course, grants Congress no express power to strip people of their citizenship, whether in the exercise of the implied power to regulate foreign affairs or in the exercise of

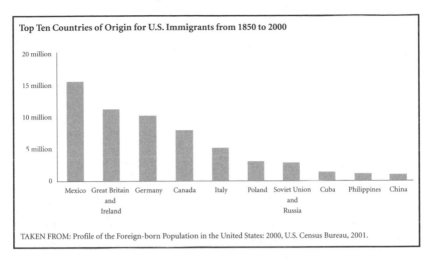

Top Ten Countries of Origin for U.S. Immigrants from 1850 to 2000

TAKEN FROM: Profile of the Foreign-born Population in the United States: 2000, U.S. Census Bureau, 2001.

any specifically granted power. And even before the adoption of the Fourteenth Amendment, views were expressed in Congress and by this Court that under the Constitution the Government was granted no power, even under its express power to pass a uniform rule of naturalization, to determine what conduct should and should not result in the loss of citizenship. . . .

## The Fourteenth Amendment Is Clear

Although these legislative and judicial statements may be regarded as inconclusive and must be considered in the historical context in which they were made, any doubt as to whether prior to the passage of the Fourteenth Amendment Congress had the power to deprive a person against his will of citizenship once obtained should have been removed by the un equivocal terms of the Amendment itself. It provides its own constitutional rule in language calculated completely to control the status of citizenship: "All persons born or naturalized in the United States . . . are citizens of the United States. . . ." There is no indication in these words of a fleeting citizenship, good at the moment it is acquired but subject to destruction by the Government at any time. Rather the Amendment can most reasonably be read as defining a citizenship which a citizen keeps unless he voluntarily relinquishes it. Once acquired, this Fourteenth Amendment citizenship was not to be shifted, canceled, or diluted at the will of the Federal Government, the States, or any other governmental unit.

It is true that the chief interest of the people in giving permanence and security to citizenship in the Fourteenth Amendment was the desire to protect Negroes. The Dred Scott decision had shortly before greatly disturbed many people about the status of Negro citizenship. But the Civil Rights Act of 1866 had already attempted to confer citizenship on all persons born or naturalized in the United States. Nevertheless, when the Fourteenth Amendment passed the House without containing any definition of citizenship, the sponsors of the Amendment in the Senate insisted on inserting a constitutional definition and grant of citizenship. They expressed fears that the citizenship so recently conferred on Negroes by the Civil Rights Act could be just as easily taken away from them by subsequent Congresses, and it was to provide an insuperable obstacle against every governmental effort to strip Negroes of their newly acquired citizenship that the first clause was added to the Fourteenth Amendment. Senator [Jacob] Howard, who sponsored the Amendment in the Senate, thus explained the purpose of the clause:

> "It settles the great question of citizenship and removes all doubt as to what persons are or are not citizens of the United States. . . . We desired to put this question of citizenship and the rights of citizens . . . under the civil rights bill beyond the legislative power. . . ."

This undeniable purpose of the Fourteenth Amendment to make citizenship of Negroes permanent and secure would be frustrated by holding that the Government can rob a citizen of his citizenship without his consent by simply proceeding to act under an implied general power to regulate foreign affairs or some other power generally granted. Though the framers of the Amendment were not particularly concerned with the problem of expatriation, it seems undeniable from the language they used that they wanted to put citizenship beyond the power of any governmental unit to destroy. In 1868, two years after the Fourteenth Amendment had been proposed, Congress specifically considered the subject of expatriation. Several bills were introduced to impose involuntary expatriation on citizens who committed certain acts. With little discussion, these proposals were defeated. Other bills, like the one proposed but defeated in 1818, provided merely a means by which the citizen could himself voluntarily renounce his citizenship. Representative Van Trump of Ohio, who proposed such a bill, vehemently denied in supporting it that his measure would make the Government "a party to the act dissolving the tie between the citizen and his country . . . where the statute simply prescribes the manner in which the citizen shall proceed to perpetuate the evidence of his intention, or election, to renounce his citizenship by expatriation." He insisted that "inasmuch as the act of expatriation depends almost entirely upon a question of intention on the part of the citizen," "the true question is, that not only the right of expatriation, but the whole power of its exercise, rests solely and exclusively in the will of the individual." In strongest of terms, not contradicted by any during the debates, he concluded:

> "To enforce expatriation or exile against a citizen without his consent is not a power anywhere belonging to this Government. No conservative-minded statesman, no intelligent legislator, no sound lawyer has ever maintained any such power in any branch of the Government. The lawless precedents created in the delirium of war . . . of sending men by force into exile, as a punishment for political opinion, were violations of this great law . . . of the Constitution. . . . The men who debated the question in 1818 failed to see the true distinction. . . . They failed to comprehend that it is not the Government, but that it is the individual, who has the right and the only power of expatriation. . . . [I]t belongs and ap-

pertains to the citizen and not to the Government; and it is the evidence of his election to exercise his right, and not the power to control either the election or the right itself, which is the legitimate subject matter of legislation. There has been, and there can be, no legislation under our Constitution to control in any manner the right itself."

But even Van Trump's proposal, which went no further than to provide a means of evidencing a citizen's intent to renounce his citizenship, was defeated. The Act, as finally passed, merely recognized the "right of expatriation" as an inherent right of all people.

The entire legislative history of the 1868 Act makes it abundantly clear that there was a strong feeling in the Congress that the only way the citizenship it conferred could be lost was by the voluntary renunciation or abandonment by the citizen himself. And this was the unequivocal statement of the Court in the case of *United States v. Wong Kim Ark*. The issues in that case were whether a person born in the United States to Chinese aliens was a citizen of the United States and whether, nevertheless, he could be excluded under the Chinese Exclusion Act. The Court first held that within the terms of the Fourteenth Amendment, Wong Kim Ark was a citizen of the United States, and then pointed out that though he might "renounce this citizenship, and become a citizen of ... any other country," he had never done so. The Court then held that Congress could not do anything to abridge or affect his citizenship conferred by the Fourteenth Amendment. Quoting Chief Justice [John] Marshall's well-considered and oft-repeated dictum in *Osborn* [*Osborn v. Bank of the United States*, 1824] to the effect that Congress under the power of naturalization has "a power to confer citizenship, not a power to take it away," the Court said:

"Congress having no power to abridge the rights conferred by the Constitution upon those who have become naturalized citizens by virtue of acts of Congress, a fortiori [by stronger reason] no act . . . of Congress . . . can affect citizenship acquired as a birthright, by virtue of the Constitution itself. . . . The Fourteenth Amendment, while it leaves the power, where it was before, in Congress, to regulate naturalization, has conferred no authority upon Congress to restrict the effect of birth, declared by the Constitution to constitute a sufficient and complete right to citizenship."

To uphold Congress' power to take away a man's citizenship because he voted in a foreign election in violation of 401(e) would be equivalent to holding that Congress has the power to "abridge," "affect," "restrict the effect of," and "take . . . away" citizenship. Because the Fourteenth Amendment prevents Congress from doing any of these things, we agree with THE CHIEF JUSTICE'S dissent in the Perez case that the Government is without power to rob a citizen of his citizenship under 401(e).

Because the legislative history of the Fourteenth Amendment and of the expatriation proposals which preceded and followed it, like most other legislative history, contains many statements from which conflicting inferences can be drawn, our holding might be unwarranted if it rested entirely or principally upon that legislative history. But it does not. Our holding we think is the only one that can stand in view of the language and the purpose of the Fourteenth Amendment, and our construction of that Amendment, we believe, comports more nearly than *Perez* with the principles of liberty and equal justice to all that the entire Fourteenth Amendment was adopted to guarantee. Citizenship is no light trifle to be jeopardized any moment Congress decides to do so under the name of one of its general or implied grants of power. In some instances, loss of citizenship can mean that a man is left without the protection of citizenship in any country in the world—as a man without a country. Citizenship in this Nation is a part of a cooperative affair. Its citizenry is the country and the country is its citizenry. The very nature of our free government makes it completely incongruous to have a rule of law under which a group of citizens temporarily in office can deprive another group of citizens of their citizenship. We hold that the Fourteenth Amendment was designed to, and does, protect every citizen of this Nation against a congressional forcible destruction of his citizenship, whatever his creed, color, or race. Our holding does no more than to give to this citizen that which is his own, a constitutional right to remain a citizen in a free country unless he voluntarily relinquishes that citizenship.

*Perez v. Brownell* is overruled. The [earlier, lower court] judgment is Reversed.

# The Fourteenth Amendment Does Not Guarantee Citizenship in All Circumstances

*John Marshall Harlan*

*The following selection is taken from Supreme Court Justice John Marshall Harlan's dissent in the* Afroyim v. Rusk *decision, which declared that the plaintiff, Beys Afroyim, did not forfeit his U.S. citizenship by voting in a foreign election, because his citizenship was guaranteed by the Fourteenth Amendment and he had shown no willingness to give it up. Harlan rejects the majority's argument that Congress does not have the right to remove an American's citizenship without his or her consent, and to do so he cites numerous legislative and judicial precedents where Congress has indeed exercised that right. The most recent of these was in* Perez v. Brownell *(1958), where the Supreme Court de cided that an American citizen living in Mexico had forfeited his citizenship by voting in Mexican elections.*

*For Harlan, the Fourteenth Amendment's citizenship guarantees were not necessarily relevant in this case. He claims that "nothing in the history, purposes, or language of the clause suggests that it forbids Congress in all circumstances to withdraw the citizenship of an unwilling citizen." Harlan argues that by voting in a foreign election, Afroyim had shown that he was "an unwilling citizen."*

M R. JUSTICE HARLAN, whom MR. JUSTICE CLARK, MR. JUSTICE STEWART, and MR. JUSTICE WHITE join, dissenting.

Almost 10 years ago, in *Perez v. Brownell*, the Court upheld the constitutionality of 401 (e) of the Nationality Act of 1940. The section deprives of his nationality any citizen who

John Marshall Harlan, *"Afroyim v. Rusk,"* in U.S. Supreme Court, 387 U.S. 253 (1967), May 1967.

has voted in a foreign political election. The Court reasoned that Congress derived from its power to regulate foreign affairs authority to expatriate any citizen who intentionally commits acts which may be prejudicial to the foreign relations of the United States, and which reasonably may be deemed to indicate a dilution of his allegiance to this country. Congress, it was held, could appropriately consider purposeful voting in a foreign political election to be such an act.

The Court today overrules *Perez*, and declares 401 (e) unconstitutional, by a remarkable process of circumlocution. First, the Court fails almost entirely to dispute the reasoning in *Perez*; it is essentially content with the conclusory and quite unsubstantiated assertion that Congress is without "any general power, express or implied," to expatriate a citizen "without his assent." Next, the Court embarks upon a lengthy, albeit incomplete, survey of the historical background of the congressional power at stake here, and yet, at the end, concedes that the history is susceptible of "conflicting inferences." The Court acknowledges that its conclusions might not be warranted by that history alone, and disclaims that the decision today relies, even "principally," upon it. Finally, the Court declares that its result is bottomed upon the "language and the purpose" of the Citizenship Clause of the Fourteenth Amendment; in explanation, the Court offers only the terms of the clause itself, the contention that any other result would be "completely incongruous," and the essentially arcane observation that the "citizenry is the country and the country is its citizenry."

I can find nothing in this extraordinary series of circumventions which permits, still less compels, the imposition of this constitutional constraint upon the authority of Congress. I must respectfully dissent. . . .

In the spring and summer of 1864, both Houses debated intensively the Wade-Davis bill to provide reconstruction governments for the States which had seceded to form the Confederacy. Among the bill's provisions was 14, by which "every person who shall hereafter hold or exercise any office . . . in the rebel service . . . is hereby declared not to be a citizen of the United States." Much of the debate upon the bill did not, of course, center on the expatriation provision, although it certainly did not escape critical attention. Nonetheless, I have not found any indication in the debates in either House that it was supposed that Congress was without authority to deprive an unwilling citizen of his citizenship. The bill was not signed by President Lincoln before the adjournment of Congress, and thus failed to become law, but a subsequent statement issued by Lincoln makes quite plain that he was not troubled by any doubts of the constitutionality of 14. Passage of the Wade-Davis bill of itself "suffices to destroy the notion that the men who drafted the Fourteenth Amendment felt that citizenship was an 'absolute.'"

## Congress Tried to Withdraw Citizenship Before

Twelve months later, and less than a year before its passage of the Fourteenth Amendment, Congress adopted a second measure which included provisions that permitted the expatriation of unwilling citizens. Section 21 of the Enrollment Act of 1865 provided that deserters from the military service of the United States "shall be deemed and taken to have voluntarily relinquished and forfeited their rights of citizenship and their rights to become citizens. . . ." The same section extended these disabilities to persons who departed the United States with intent to avoid "draft into the military or naval service. . . ." The bitterness of war did not cause Congress here to neglect the requirements of the Constitution; for it was urged in both Houses that 21 as written was ex post facto [after the fact], thus was constitutionally impermissible. Significantly, however, it was never suggested in either debate that expatriation without a citizen's consent lay beyond Congress' authority. Members of both Houses had apparently examined intensively the section's constitutional validity, and yet had been undisturbed by the matters upon which the Court now relies.

Some doubt, based on the phrase "rights of citizenship," has since been expressed that 21 was intended to require any more than disfranchisement, but this is, for several reasons, unconvincing. First, 21 also explicitly provided that persons subject to its provisions should not thereafter exercise various "rights of citizens"; if the section had not been intended to cause expatriation, it is difficult to see why these additional provisions would have been thought necessary. Second, the executive authorities of the United States afterwards consistently construed the section as causing expatriation. Third, the section was apparently understood by various courts to result in expatriation; in particular, Mr. Justice Strong, while a member of the Supreme Court of Pennsylvania, construed the section to cause a "forfeiture of citizenship," and although this point was not expressly reached, his general understanding of the statute was approved by this Court in *Kurtz v. Moffit* [an 1885 decision that prevented state police officers from arresting federal criminals without warrants]. Finally, Congress in 1867 approved an exemption from the section's provisions for those who had deserted after the termination of general hostilities, and the statute as adopted specifically described the disability from which exemption was given as a "loss of his citizenship." The same choice of phrase occurs in the pertinent debates.

It thus appears that Congress had twice, immediately before its passage of the Fourteenth Amendment, unequivocally affirmed its belief that it had authority to expatriate an unwilling citizen. . . .

## The Fourteenth Amendment Is Not Relevant Here

The evidence with which the Court supports its thesis that the Citizenship Clause of the Fourteenth Amendment was intended to lay at rest any doubts of Congress' inability to expatriate without the citizen's consent is no more persuasive. The evidence consists almost exclusively of two brief and general quotations from [Sen. Jacob] Howard of Michigan, the sponsor of the Citizenship Clause in the Senate, and of a statement made in a debate in the House of Representatives in 1868 by [Philadelphia] Van Trump of Ohio. Measured most generously, this evidence would be inadequate to support the important constitutional conclusion presumably drawn in large part from it by the Court; but, as will be shown, other relevant evidence indicates that the Court plainly has mistaken the purposes of the clause's draftsmen.

The Amendment as initially approved by the House contained nothing which described or defined citizenship. The issue did not as such even arise in the House debates; it was apparently assumed that Negroes were citizens, and that it was necessary only to guarantee to them the rights which sprang from citizenship. It is quite impossible to derive from these debates any indication that the House wished to deny itself the authority it had exercised in 1864 and 1865; so far as the House is concerned, it seems that no issues of citizenship were "at all involved."

In the Senate, however, it was evidently feared that unless citizenship were defined, or some more general classification substituted, freedmen might, on the premise that they were not citizens, be excluded from the Amendment's protection. Senator [William] Stewart thus offered an amendment which would have inserted into [section] 1 a definition of citizenship, and Senator [Benjamin] Wade urged as an alternative the elimination of the term "citizen" from the Amendment's first section. After a caucus of the chief supporters of the Amendment, Senator Howard announced on their behalf that they favored the addition of the present Citizenship Clause. . . .

Further, the executive authorities of the United States repeatedly acted, in the 40 years following 1868, upon the premise that a citizen might automatically be deemed to have expatriated himself by conduct short of a voluntary renunciation of citizenship; individual citizens were, as the Court indicated in *Perez*, regularly held on this basis to have lost their citizenship. Interested Members of Congress, and others, could scarcely have been unaware of the practice; as early as 1874, President [Ulysses S.] Grant urged Congress in his Sixth Annual Message to supplement the Act of 1868 with a statutory declaration of the acts by which a citizen might "be deemed to have renounced or to have lost his citizenship." It was the necessity to provide a more satisfactory basis for this practice that led first to the appointment of the Citizenship Board of 1906, and subsequently to the Nationality Acts of 1907 and 1940 [all of which tried to refine the understanding of citizenship]. The administrative practice in this period was described by the Court in *Perez*; it suffices here merely to emphasize that the Court today has not ventured to explain why the Citizenship Clause should, so shortly after its adoption, have been, under the Court's construction, so seriously misunderstood.

It seems to me apparent that the historical evidence which the Court in part recites is wholly inconclusive, as indeed the Court recognizes; the evidence, to the contrary, irresistibly suggests that the draftsmen of the Fourteenth Amendment did not intend, and could not have expected, that the Citizenship Clause would deprive Congress of authority which it had, to their knowledge, only recently twice exercised. The construction demanded by the pertinent historical evidence, and entirely consistent with the clause's terms and purposes, is instead that it declares to whom citizenship, as a consequence either of birth or of naturalization, initially attaches. The clause thus served at the time of its passage both to overturn Dred Scott and to provide a foundation for federal citizenship entirely independent of state citizenship; in this fashion it effectively guaranteed that the Amendment's protection would not subsequently be withheld from those for whom it was principally intended. But nothing in the history, purposes, or language of the clause suggests that it forbids Congress in all circumstances to withdraw the citizenship of an unwilling citizen. To the contrary, it was expected, and should now be understood, to leave Congress at liberty to expatriate a citizen if the expatriation is an appropriate exercise of a power otherwise given to Congress by the Constitution, and if the methods and terms of expatriation adopted by Congress are consistent with the Constitution's other relevant commands.

The Citizenship Clause thus neither denies nor provides to Congress any power of expatriation; its consequences are, for present purposes, exhausted by its declaration of the classes of individuals to whom citizenship initially attaches. Once obtained, citizenship is of course protected from arbitrary withdrawal by the constraints placed around Congress' powers by the Constitution; it is not proper to create from the Citizenship Clause an additional, and entirely unwarranted, restriction upon legislative authority. The construction now placed on the Citizenship Clause rests, in the last analysis, simply on the Court's *ipse dixit* [unsupported assertion], evincing little more, it is quite apparent, than the present majority's own distaste for the expatriation power.

I believe that *Perez* was rightly decided, and on its authority would affirm the judgment of the Court of Appeals.

# Individual States Cannot Deny Public Education to the Children of Undocumented Immigrants

*William Brennan*

*As a result of changes to its immigration laws beginning in 1965, the United States began to see increasing numbers of newcomers from other countries in the next decades. While most immigrants entered the country legally, many did not. Among those undocumented immigrants were Europeans who overstayed tourist visas and Asians who abused work visas. But the greatest number were Latin Americans, most notably Mexicans who could relatively easily cross the 2,000-mile border the Mexico shares with the United States. Indeed, these "illegal aliens" are concentrated in border states such as Texas, Arizona, and California.*

*The presence of these large groups of undocumented immigrants has been and continues to be the source of much controversy over what public rights and services such immigrants can expect to enjoy. The following selection is taken from a 1982 Supreme Court case in which the Court determined that the State of Texas could not deny public education to children living there, even if those children were illegal immigrants themselves or if they were uncertain of their citizenship status (if the children were born on U.S. soil, they received automatic citizenship under the Fourteenth Amendment). The author of the opinion, Justice William Brennan, cited the equal protection clause of the Fourteenth Amendment in asserting that all residents of Texas were "persons" eligible for certain protections, as well as the citizenship clause in claiming that the State of Texas was not free to limit a "person's" rights.*

William Brennan, "*Plyler v. Doe*," in U.S. Supreme Court, 457 U.S. 202 (1982), June 1982.

# H*eld:*

A Texas statute which withholds from local school districts any state funds for the education of children who were not "legally admitted" into the United States, and which authorizes local school districts to deny enrollment to such children, violates the Equal Protection Clause of the Fourteenth Amendment.

(a) The illegal aliens who are plaintiffs in these cases challenging the statute may claim the benefit of the Equal Protection Clause, which provides that no State shall "deny to any person within its jurisdiction the equal protection of the laws." Whatever his status under the immigration laws, an alien is a "person" in any ordinary sense of that term. This Court's prior cases recognizing that illegal aliens are "persons" protected by the Due Process Clauses of the Fifth and Fourteenth Amendments, which Clauses do not include the phrase "within its jurisdiction," cannot be distinguished on the asserted ground that persons who have entered the country illegally are not "within the jurisdiction" of a State even if they are present within its boundaries and subject to its laws. Nor do the logic and history of the Fourteenth Amendment support such a construction. Instead, use of the phrase "within its jurisdiction" confirms the understanding that the Fourteenth Amendment's protection extends to anyone, citizen or stranger, who is subject to the laws of a State, and reaches into every corner of a State's territory.

(b) The discrimination contained in the Texas statute cannot be considered rational unless it furthers some substantial goal of the State. Although undocumented resident aliens cannot be treated as a "suspect class," and although education is not a "fundamental right," so as to require the State to justify the statutory classification by showing that it serves a compelling governmental interest, nevertheless the Texas statute imposes a lifetime hardship on a discrete class of children not accountable for their disabling status. These children can neither affect their parents' conduct nor their own undocumented status. The deprivation of public education is not like the deprivation of some other governmental benefit. Public education has a pivotal role in maintaining the fabric of our society and in sustaining our political and cultural heritage; the deprivation of education takes an inestimable toll on the social, economic, intellectual, and psychological well-being of the individual, and poses an obstacle to individual achievement. In determining the rationality of the Texas statute, its costs to the Nation and to the innocent children may properly be considered.

(c) The undocumented status of these children *vel non* [or not] does not establish a sufficient rational basis for denying them benefits that the State affords other residents. It is true that when faced with an equal protection challenge respecting a State's differential treatment of aliens, the courts must be attentive to congressional policy concerning aliens. But in the area of special constitutional sensitivity presented by these cases, and in the absence of any contrary indication fairly discernible in the legislative record, no national policy is perceived that might justify the State in denying these children an elementary education.

(d) Texas' statutory classification cannot be sustained as furthering its interest in the "preservation of the state's limited resources for the education of its lawful residents." While the State might have an interest in mitigating potentially harsh economic effects from an influx of illegal immigrants, the Texas statute does not offer an effective method of dealing with the problem. Even assuming that the net impact of illegal aliens on the economy is negative, charging tuition to undocumented children constitutes an ineffectual attempt to stem the tide of illegal immigration, at least when compared with the alternative of prohibiting employment of illegal aliens. Nor is there any merit to the suggestion that undocumented children are appropriately singled out for exclusion because of the special burdens they impose on the State's ability to provide high-quality public education. The record does not show that exclusion of undocumented children is likely to improve the overall quality of education in the State. Neither is there any merit to the claim that undocumented children are appropriately singled out because their unlawful presence within the United States renders them less likely than other children to remain within the State's boundaries and to put their education to productive social or political use within the State. . . .

JUSTICE BRENNAN delivered the opinion of the Court.

The question presented by these cases is whether, consistent with the Equal Protection Clause of the Fourteenth Amendment, Texas may deny to undocumented school-age children the free public education that it provides to children who are citizens of the United States or legally admitted aliens.

Since the late 19th century, the United States has restricted immigration into this country. Unsanctioned entry into the United States is a crime, and those who have entered unlawfully are subject to deportation. But despite the existence of these legal restrictions, a substantial number of persons have succeeded in unlawfully entering the United States, and now live within various States, including the State of Texas.

In May 1975, the Texas Legislature revised its education laws to withhold from local school districts any state funds for the education of children who were not "legally admitted" into the United States. The 1975 revision also authorized local school districts to deny enrollment in their public schools to children not "legally admitted" to the country. These cases involve constitutional challenges to those provisions.

## Plyler v. Doe

This is a class action, filed in the United States District Court for the Eastern District of Texas in September 1977, on behalf of certain school-age children of Mexican origin residing in Smith County, Tex., who could not establish that they had been legally admitted into the United States. The action complained of the exclusion of plaintiff children from the public schools of the Tyler Independent School District. The Superintendent and members of the Board of Trustees of the School District were named as defendants; the State of Texas intervened as a party-defendant. After certifying a class consisting of all undocumented school-age children of Mexican origin residing within the School District, the District Court preliminarily enjoined defendants from denying a free education to members of the plaintiff class. In December 1977, the court conducted an extensive hearing on plaintiffs' motion for permanent injunctive relief.

In considering this motion, the District Court made extensive findings of fact. The court found that neither 21.031 [the original Texas statute denying public education to illegal immigrants] nor the School District policy implementing it had "either the purpose or effect of keeping illegal aliens out of the State of Texas." Respecting defendants' further claim that 21.031 was simply a financial measure designed to avoid a drain on the State's fisc [finances], the court recognized that the increases in population resulting from the immigration of Mexican nationals into the United States had created problems for the public schools of the State, and that these problems were exacerbated by the special educational needs of immigrant Mexican children. The court noted, however, that the increase in school enrollment was primarily attributable to the admission of children who were legal residents. It also found that while the "exclusion of all undocumented children from the public schools in Texas would eventually result in economies at some level," funding from both the State and Federal Governments was based primarily on the number of children enrolled. In net effect then, barring undocumented children from the schools would save money, but it would "not necessarily" improve "the quality of education." The court further observed that the impact of 21.031 was borne primarily by a very small subclass of illegal aliens, "entire families who have migrated illegally and—for all practical purposes—permanently to the United States." Finally, the court noted that under current laws and practices "the illegal alien of today may well be the legal alien of tomorrow," and that without an education, these undocumented children, "[a]lready disadvantaged as a result of poverty, lack of English-speaking ability, and undeniable racial prejudices, . . . will become permanently locked into the lowest socio-economic class."

The District Court held that illegal aliens were entitled to the protection of the Equal Protection Clause of the Fourteenth Amendment, and that 21.031 violated that Clause. Suggesting that "the state's exclusion of undocumented children from its public schools . . . may well be the type of invidiously motivated state action for which the suspect classification doctrine was designed," the court held that it was unnecessary to decide whether the statute would survive a "strict scrutiny" analysis because, in any event, the discrimination embodied in the statute was not supported by a rational basis. The District Court also concluded that the Texas statute violated the Supremacy Clause. . . .

## Undocumented Immigrants Are Included in the Constitution

The Fourteenth Amendment provides that "[n]o State shall . . . deprive any person of life, liberty, or property, without due process of law; nor deny to any person within its jurisdiction the equal protection of the laws." Appellants argue at the outset that undocumented aliens, because of their immigration status, are not "persons within the jurisdiction" of the State of Texas, and that they therefore have no right to the equal protection of Texas law. We reject this argument. Whatever his status under the immigration laws, an alien is surely a "person" in any ordinary sense of that term. Aliens, even aliens whose presence in this country is unlawful, have long been recognized as "persons" guaranteed due process of law by the

Fifth and Fourteenth Amendments. Indeed, we have clearly held that the Fifth Amendment protects aliens whose presence in this country is unlawful from invidious discrimination by the Federal Government.

Appellants seek to distinguish our prior cases, emphasizing that the Equal Protection Clause directs a State to afford its protection to persons within its jurisdiction while the Due Process Clauses of the Fifth and Fourteenth Amendments contain no such assertedly limiting phrase. In appellants' view, persons who have entered the United States illegally are not "within the jurisdiction" of a State even if they are present within a State's boundaries and subject to its laws. Neither our cases nor the logic of the Fourteenth Amendment supports that constricting construction of the phrase "within its jurisdiction." We have never suggested that the class of persons who might avail themselves of the equal protection guarantee is less than coextensive with that entitled to due process. To the contrary, we have recognized that both provisions were fashioned to protect an identical class of persons, and to reach every exercise of state authority.

> "The Fourteenth Amendment to the Constitution is not confined to the protection of citizens. It says: 'Nor shall any state deprive any person of life, liberty, or property without due process of law; nor deny to any person within its jurisdiction the equal protection of the laws.' These provisions are universal in their application, to all persons within the territorial jurisdiction, without regard to any differences of race, of color, or of nationality; and the protection of the laws is a pledge of the protection of equal laws."

In concluding that "all persons within the territory of the United States," including aliens unlawfully present, may invoke the Fifth and Sixth Amendments to challenge actions of the Federal Government, we reasoned from the understanding that the Fourteenth Amendment was designed to afford its protection to all within the boundaries of a State. Our cases applying the Equal Protection Clause reflect the same territorial theme.

> "Manifestly, the obligation of the State to give the protection of equal laws can be performed only where its laws operate, that is, within its own jurisdiction. It is there that the equality of legal right must be maintained. That obligation is imposed by the Constitution upon the States severally as governmental entities, each responsible for its own laws establishing the rights and duties of persons within its borders."

There is simply no support for appellants' suggestion that "due process" is somehow of greater stature than "equal protection" and therefore available to a larger class of persons. To the contrary, each aspect of the Fourteenth Amendment reflects an elementary limitation on state power. To permit a State to employ the phrase "within its jurisdiction" in order to identify subclasses of persons whom it would define as beyond its jurisdiction, thereby relieving itself of the obligation to assure that its laws are designed and applied equally to those persons, would undermine the principal purpose for which the Equal Protection Clause was incorporated in the Fourteenth Amendment. The Equal Protection Clause was intended to work nothing less than the abolition of all caste-based and invidious class-based legislation. That objective is fundamentally at odds with the power the State asserts here to classify persons subject to its laws as nonetheless excepted from its protection.

Although the congressional debate concerning [section] 1 of the Fourteenth Amendment was limited, that debate clearly confirms the understanding that the phrase "within its jurisdiction" was intended in a broad sense to offer the guarantee of equal protection to all within a State's boundaries, and to all upon whom the State would impose the obligations of its laws. Indeed, it appears from those debates that Congress, by using the phrase "person within its jurisdiction," sought expressly to ensure that the equal protection of the laws was provided to the alien population. Representative [John] Bingham reported to the House the draft resolution of the Joint Committee of Fifteen on Reconstruction that was to become the Fourteenth Amendment. Two days later, Bingham posed the following question in support of the resolution:

> "Is it not essential to the unity of the people that the citizens of each State shall be entitled to all the privileges and immunities of citizens in the several States? Is it not essential to the unity of the Government and the unity of the people that all persons, whether citizens or strangers, within this land, shall have equal protection in every State in this Union in the rights of life and liberty and property?"

Senator [Jacob] Howard, also a member of the Joint Committee of Fifteen [charged with establishing Reconstruction policy], and the floor manager of the Amendment in the Senate, was no less explicit about the broad objectives of the Amendment, and the intention to make its provisions applicable to all who "may happen to be" within the jurisdiction of a State:

> "The last two clauses of the first section of the amendment disable a State from depriving not merely a citizen of the United States, but any person, whoever he may be, of life, liberty, or property without due process of law, or from denying to him the equal protection of the laws of the State. This abolishes all class legislation in the States and does away with the injustice of subjecting one caste of persons to a code not applicable to another. . . . It will, if adopted by the States, forever disable every one of them from passing laws trenching upon those fundamental rights and privileges which pertain to citizens of the United States, and to all persons who may happen to be within their jurisdiction."

Use of the phrase "within its jurisdiction" thus does not detract from, but rather confirms, the understanding that the

*A twelve-year-old boy, who is an illegal immigrant from El Salvador, works on a school paper at a community outreach center for Hispanic immigrants in California.* AP Images.

protection of the Fourteenth Amendment extends to anyone, citizen or stranger, who is subject to the laws of a State, and reaches into every corner of a State's territory. That a person's initial entry into a State, or into the United States, was unlawful, and that he may for that reason be expelled, cannot negate the simple fact of his presence within the State's territorial perimeter. Given such presence, he is subject to the full range of obligations imposed by the State's civil and criminal laws. And until he leaves the jurisdiction—either voluntarily, or involuntarily in accordance with the Constitution and laws of the United States—he is entitled to the equal protection of the laws that a State may choose to establish.

CONSTITUTIONAL
AMENDMENTS
BEYOND THE BILL OF RIGHTS

CHAPTER 3

# Citizenship Controversies in Contemporary America

# The Fourteenth Amendment's Guarantee of Birthright Citizenship Should Be Changed

*Ron Paul*

*One of the unintended consequences of the citizenship clause of the Fourteenth Amendment was that it granted automatic citizenship to the children of recent immigrants to the United States, even if those immigrants came to the United States illegally. The proponents of the Fourteenth Amendment, focusing on guaranteeing citizenship for freed slaves, did not foresee the massive immigration that was to begin in the late nineteenth century and continue, with some breaks, until the present day. Nor did they consider that so many immigrants would enter the United States illegally; at the time there were no meaningful immigration restrictions that would-be newcomers might flout.*

*The following selection, written by Texas congressman Ron Paul, presents the argument that the right of automatic citizenship by birth should be reconsidered. Paul notes that the United States is no longer a country of empty spaces and wide frontiers. He also claims that the nation's welfare system is one of the chief draws for undocumented immigrants.*

*Ron Paul has represented south Texas congressional districts off and on since the 1970s. The area is, as he claims, a region with a major concentration of recent immigrants, both legal and illegal. His 2008 candidacy for the Republican nomination for U.S. president received a great deal of unexpected interest.*

A recent article in the *Houston Chronicle* discusses the problem of so-called anchor babies, children born in U.S. hospitals to illegal immigrant parents. These children

Ron Paul, "Rethinking Birthright Citizenship," LewRockwell.com, October 3, 2006. Reproduced by permission of the publisher and author.

*Republican Congressman Ron Paul of Texas.* ©Michal Czerwonka/epa/Corbis.

automatically become citizens, and thus serve as an anchor for their parents to remain in the country. Our immigration authorities understandably are reluctant to break up families by deporting parents of young babies. But birthright citizenship, originating in the 14th amendment, has become a serious cultural and economic dilemma for our nation.

In some Houston hospitals, administrators estimate that 70 or 80% of the babies born have parents who are in the country illegally. As an obstetrician in south Texas for several decades, I can attest to the severity of the problem. It's the same story in California, Arizona, and New Mexico. And the truth is most illegal immigrants who have babies in U.S. hospitals do not have health insurance and do not pay their hospital bills.

This obviously cannot be sustained, either by the hospitals involved or the taxpayers who end up paying the bills.

No other wealthy, western nations grant automatic citizenship to those who simply happen to be born within their borders to non-citizens. These nations recognize that citizenship involves more than the physical location of one's birth; it also involves some measure of cultural connection and allegiance. In most cases this means the parents must be citizens of a nation in order for their newborn children to receive automatic citizenship.

Make no mistake, Americans are happy to welcome immigrants who follow our immigration laws and seek a better life here. America is far more welcoming and tolerant of newcomers than virtually any nation on earth. But our modern welfare state creates perverse incentives for immigrants, incentives that cloud the issue of why people choose to come here. The real problem is not immigration, but rather the welfare state magnet.

## Unfair Burdens on the State

Hospitals bear the costs when illegal immigrants enter the country for the express purpose of giving birth. But illegal immigrants also use emergency rooms, public roads, and public schools. In many cases they are able to obtain Medicaid, food stamps, public housing, and even unemployment benefits. Some have fraudulently collected Social Security benefits.

Of course many American citizens also use or abuse the welfare system. But we cannot afford to open our pocketbooks to the rest of the world. We must end the perverse incentives that encourage immigrants to come here illegally, including the anchor baby incentive.

I've introduced legislation that would amend the Constitution and end automatic birthright citizenship. The 14th amendment was ratified in 1868, on the heels of the Civil War. The country, especially the western territories, was wide open and ripe for homesteading. There was no welfare state to exploit, and the modern problems associated with immigration could not have been imagined.

Our founders knew that unforeseen problems with our system of government would arise, and that's precisely why they gave us a method for amending the Constitution. It's time to rethink birthright citizenship by amending the 14th amendment.

# Current Debates over Citizenship for Immigrants Recall Arguments from Earlier Times

*Garrett Epps*

*In the following selection, writer Garrett Epps takes issue with those who would argue that the Fourteenth Amendment's guarantee of citizenship for all should be reconsidered. He claims that it should instead be celebrated. The Fourteenth Amendment ensured that all Americans, including immigrants, enjoyed equal rights and legal protections, and it prevented the individual states from limiting those privileges. Epps also notes that many of the arguments in favor of lifting birthright citizenship for immigrants or their children are based on the belief that recent immigrants will cling to their old ways and refuse to assimilate. But, as he recognizes, anti-immigrant forces made the same arguments about such earlier newcomers as the millions of Germans and Irish who came to the United States in the mid-1800s. Garrett Epps teaches constitutional law at the University of Oregon. He has also worked as a reporter for the* Washington Post.

What's better than a patriotic holiday in July? Pop a brew tonight, then, and let's celebrate our heritage of democracy and equal rights. We owe these freedoms not so much to the events commemorated every July 4, but to those of July 21.

On this day in 1868, after a bruising ratification struggle, Congress passed a resolution proclaiming that the 14th Amendment was part of the Constitution. More than the Dec-

Garrett Epps, "Happy 14th Amendment Day!" Salon.com, July 21, 2006. This article first appeared in Salon.com, at http://www.salon.com. An online version remains in the Salon archives. Reprinted with permission.

laration of Independence, more than the original Constitution, more than even the Bill of Rights, it is the 14th Amendment that makes America a democratic country.

But, as the beer commercials say, celebrate responsibly: Our current toxic immigration debate shows that, more than a century later, genuine democracy has powerful enemies. In 2006, the anti-immigrant movement is attacking the amendment's central meaning of equal protection of the law for all.

Please don't feel bad if the words "14th Amendment" don't immediately call to mind a list of rights. Most literate citizens—and even many lawyers—have trouble focusing on the radical changes this massive post-Civil War reform made in the original Constitution. The 14th Amendment is such a giant presence in our lives today that it's hard to see it as a single thing.

But consider this. Until the 14th Amendment, the idea of human equality, extolled in the Declaration of Independence, appeared nowhere in the Constitution. The word "equal," when written in the original document, referred mostly to voting privileges for the states. In addition, the Constitution contained no definition of American citizenship, seemingly leaving the matter to the states.

Even the Bill of Rights itself only covered the federal government—overreaching state governments could, and did, restrict free speech, freedom of religion, due process of law and other basic rights. In short, the Framers of 1787 set up a flawed confederation of insular states, each of which was free to oppress, and even enslave, some or all of its population.

No matter what we've been taught in civics class, that original system was a failure. Its flaws led directly to the bloodiest war in American history. After nearly a million deaths, the anti-slavery leaders of Congress set out in 1865 to re-create the United States as a nation, with a powerful central government, democratic institutions at every level and a list of

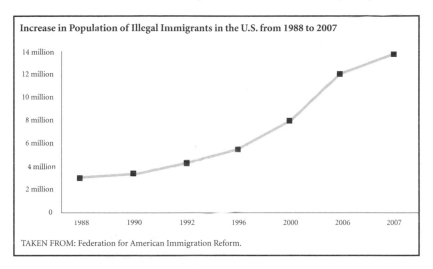

Increase in Population of Illegal Immigrants in the U.S. from 1988 to 2007

TAKEN FROM: Federation for American Immigration Reform.

rights no government, state or federal, could violate. Far more than the Framers of 1787, John Bingham, Thaddeus Stevens, William P. Fessenden and the other authors of the 14th Amendment designed the America we live in today. It was, in their vision, to be a unified nation. Local majorities in states were to be barred by federal power from oppressing religious, political or racial minorities. And immigrants were to be a part of the nation as fully as those native-born, considered equal before the courts.

## The Fourteenth Amendment Helped Create Modern America

The concerns that motivated them seem, even 140 years later, remarkably contemporary. The first section of the amendment begins by guaranteeing that "all persons born or naturalized in the United States, and subject to the jurisdiction thereof, are citizens of the United States and of the State wherein they reside." At one stroke, the framers eliminated the racist Dred Scott doctrine that "we the people" did not mean African-Americans; and they included as citizens every child born here, no matter where their parents were born or how they got here. After that, they required every state to observe the "privileges [and] immunities of citizens of the United States," and to afford due process and equal protection of the laws to "any person" within their borders.

Ohio Rep. John Bingham, the principal architect of Section 1, had spent most of his career campaigning for the rights of slaves and immigrants. Even before the Civil War, he had laid out a vision of "one people, one Constitution, and one country!" States had no "rights" to interfere with their citizens' constitutional rights: "The equality of the right to live; the right to know; to argue and to utter, according to conscience; to work and enjoy the product of their toil, is the rock on which [the] Constitution rests, its sure foundation and defense." Immigrants enjoyed those rights as fully as natives, he insisted, because the Constitution obeyed "that higher law given by a voice out of heaven: 'Ye shall have the same law for the stranger as for one of your own country.'"

The bedrock values of birthright citizenship and equal protection for all immigrants came directly out of the debates over immigration of the 1850s—debates that sound remarkably like the one going on in Congress today. By 1860, German-born immigrants to the United States totaled 1.2 million out of about 30 million total, and thousands of Irish immigrants were arriving yearly. Prophets of the "Know Nothing" movement [a political group that opposed immigration in the 1850s] warned that these new immigrants were not like previous ones. They did not assimilate; they owed allegiance to the pope; they insisted on speaking their own languages; they would subvert American institutions and destroy American identity.

Even worse, they drank beer.

Many proposals were floated to restrict their rights, requiring 21 years for citizenship or withholding the vote entirely. But anti-slavery Republicans like Bingham insisted that a free republic did not deal in hierarchies of rights.

Today's Know-Nothings are attempting to avoid this central tenet of American democracy by deliberately distorting the meaning of the 14th Amendment. On its Web site, the anti-immigrant Federation for American Immigration Reform dismisses the Citizenship Clause by saying it "was intended to exclude from automatic citizenship American-born persons whose allegiance to the United States was not complete"—including illegal immigrants.

## Changing the Citizenship Clause

But there is no shred of evidence in the record to support this strained interpretation. The wording of the clause was designed to exclude from citizenship chiefly the children of diplomats living in the United States under the protection of their countries of origin. And the proponents were utterly clear that birthright citizenship would reach American-born Chinese (whose parents were barred from naturalization) and Mexicans in the Southwest. And while there were no "illegal immigrants" in 1866, anti-immigrant congressmen did warn that the 14th Amendment would extend citizenship to one group that they described very similarly. Democratic Rep. Edgar Cowan warned that the U.S. had been invaded by aliens "who owe to [the U.S. government] no allegiance; who pretend to owe none; who recognize no authority in her government; who have a distinct, independent government of their own—an imperium in imperio ["state within a state"]; who pay no taxes; who never perform military service; who do nothing, in fact, which becomes the citizen, and perform none of the duties which devolve upon him."

These terrifying intruders were the Roma, or Gypsy people.

Sponsors of the amendment predicted that the United States would survive Gypsy citizenship; and so it has, just as it survived German, Irish, Italian, Jewish and other immigrants, and as it will survive immigration by Spanish-speaking people from Mexico and elsewhere. History shows that new waves of immigration pose far less danger to America than do new efforts to cut back on democracy, or to institute new classes of citizens with, as the Supreme Court said in Dred Scott, "no rights a white man [is] bound to respect."

Sometime between 1860 and today, beer stopped being an alien danger and became an American institution. So today, if you or your parents came to this country from another and gained citizenship; if your family moved from one state to another and received equal treatment in your new home; if you benefit from laws forbidding racial discrimination by government; if you are glad that your local cops can't arrest you without a warrant and torture you until you "confess" to a crime; if you don't think censorship of the news by state and local government is a good idea; if you don't want Jim Sensenbrenner and Tom Tancredo [politicians favoring strong measures against illegal immigrants] deciding whether your American-born children "deserve" citizenship—then lift a stein to the 14th Amendment and the far-seeing legislators who wrote it.

Fireworks are appropriate on national holidays. But those who would dismantle our basic constitutional guarantees are playing with real fire. The history they want to repeat—the imposition of a hereditary, lifelong, racial caste system—was tragic, and a new system of permanent aliens would be no less so. Our best weapon against this evil is knowledge of our own history and values.

# Illegal Immigrants Abuse the Fourteenth Amendment by Having Babies in the United States

*Dmitri Vasillaros*

*Among the main arguments made in recent years by those who oppose the Fourteenth Amendment's citizenship clause is the claim that it makes possible the birth of "anchor babies." These are children whose parents came to the United States illegally, but who are provided with U.S. citizenship simply by virtue of their having been born on U.S. soil.*

*In the following selection, Pittsburgh journalist Dmitri Vasillaros examines the case of a woman who, he suspects, gave birth to a child in the United States in order to take advantage of the Fourteenth Amendment's citizenship guarantees. The child therefore became an "anchor baby" whose guaranteed U.S. citizenship provided a number of possible benefits. These included the right to use the schools and public welfare systems of the state of Illinois, where the mother and child lived. They also provided the mother, an illegal immigrant, with a stronger case for her own claims to stay in the United States. Vasillaros questions not only these rights but also the right of the child's mother to claim sanctuary by living in a church. Dmitri Vasillaros is a regular columnist for the* Pittsburgh Tribune Review.

Saul Arellano is an 8-year-old anchor baby. The American-born son of an illegal alien from Mexico also is the poster child for the stunningly disingenuous arguments of advocates for illegals. His mom—holed up in a storefront church in Chicago claiming "sanctuary" so the feds don't deport her, *again*—is better at double talk than English.

Dmitri Vasillaros, "Berthing Anchor Babies," *Pittsburgh Tribune Review*, May 20, 2007. Reproduced by permission.

A few days ago I spoke by phone with Elvira Arellano, 32, through her interpreter, Beti Guevara, an associate pastor at the Aldalberto United Methodist Church where Ms. Arellano and son have lived since August.

"Saulito (Little Saul) is an American citizen," says Arellano. "He has the right to stay in his own country. Being his mom, I have the right to stay here and take care of him."

The term "anchor baby" refers to children born in the U.S. whose parents are not citizens. Since the baby automatically is considered an American citizen, that's how an alien parent could drop anchor to berth in the child's homeland.

"For all the people that say he is an anchor, those are people who have hate, anger and are racist," she says. But she won't say anything about her child's father.

"First of all, Saulito is a child of God. This country belongs to God. If Saulito was 18 years old, I could leave but right now he can't leave his mother. He needs her in this country."

If she is deported, she says it will break up her two-person family.

And that would mean the state of Illinois no longer would provide health care for Saul, who she says sees a psychologist every week and has a hyperactive disorder. He gets A's and B's in his public school but is afraid of authority figures, mom says.

However, Saulito wasn't even a gleam in anyone's eye when Arellano first was deported from the U.S. in 1997 after attempting to cross the U.S. border with fraudulent identity documents, according to U.S. Immigration and Customs Enforcement. ICE is the largest investigative arm of the Department of Homeland Security.

The agency alleges that she illegally re-entered the U.S. and was arrested again in 2002 while working, illegally, at

*A baby sleeps under an American flag at an immigrant rally in New York City.* Stan Honda/AFP/Getty Images.

[Chicago's] O'Hare International Airport under a false Social Security number. She was convicted in federal district court of Social Security fraud and then ordered deported again.

She refused to leave and now is one of roughly 600,000 immigration fugitives living here illegally after having been ordered out.

Since "sanctuary" has no legal basis in this country, ICE says it has the authority to arrest illegal aliens in all locales. But the agency won't say what, if anything, it plans to do about Arellano. It's a Mexican standoff.

Arellano is president of United Latino Family, which claims to lobby for families facing schism by deportation. The Los Angeles-based New Sanctuary Movement credits L.A. Cardinal Roger Mahony for awakening the public and legislators to the moral and human dimensions of immigration and effectively changing the terms of the public debate, according to the *California Catholic Daily.*

But is there even *one* American standing in the way of an alien family leaving intact to return to its country of origin?

Deportation threatens unity only when a foreigner would rather be here illegally than back home preserving his family. Many Americans believe in traditional family values. It's too bad more illegals don't.

# Recent Immigrants and Their Babies Are No Threat

*Priscilla Huang*

*The Fourteenth Amendment guaranteed citizenship for all people born on U.S. soil, even if their parents live in the country illegally. In the following selection, lawyer and activist Priscilla Huang notes that some Americans either fail to believe this or want to challenge it legally. The effort to change the citizenship clause even reached the U.S. Congress in 2007.*

*Huang takes issue with one of the major contemporary arguments against the citizenship clause, which is that it provides for the birth of "anchor babies" who are alleged to be unfair burdens on America's educational and social welfare systems. She notes that, in fact, recent immigrants use social services less than long-standing citizens and in many cases face restrictions that are already in place. Nevertheless, she claims, anti-immigrant sentiments based on the fear of "anchor babies" have gone as far as attempts to target pregnant immigrants. Priscilla Huang is the Reproductive Justice Project director and Women's Law Fellow at the National Asian Pacific American Women's Forum.*

Yuki Lin, born on the stroke of midnight this New Year's, became the winner of a random drawing for a national Toys "R" Us sweepstakes. The company had promised a $25,000 U.S. savings bond to the "first American baby born in 2007." However, Yuki lost her prize after the company learned that her mother was an undocumented U.S. resident. Instead, the bond went to a baby in Gainesville, Georgia, described by her mother as "an American all the way."

The toy retailer soon found itself in the midst of the country's heated immigration debate. Under mounting pres-

Priscilla Huang, "Which Babies Are Real Americans?" TomPaine.com, February 20, 2007. Reproduced by permission.

sure, Toys "R" Us reversed its decision and awarded savings bonds to . . . three babies, including Yuki. The issue of citizenship was at the heart of this controversy: Is a baby born to undocumented immigrants an American in the same way that a baby born to non-immigrant parents is? Since the 14th Amendment grants automatic citizenship to persons born on U.S. soil, both babies have equal standing as citizens. Not all people, however, view citizenship this way. As the grandmother of the Gainesville baby told reporters, "If [the mother is] an illegal alien, that makes the baby illegal."

Today's immigration debate extends beyond the goal of limiting the rights and humanity of immigrants: It's about controlling who may be considered an American. Anti-immigrant activists contend that American citizenship is not about where you were born, but who gave birth to you. By extension, they believe—the 14th amendment notwithstanding—that the government must limit the reproductive capacities of immigrant women. Thus, immigrant women of childbearing age are central targets of unjust immigration reform policies.

## Trying to Deny Fourteenth Amendment Rights

Anti-immigrant groups, such as the Federation of American Immigration Reform (FAIR), believe immigrant women of childbearing age are a significant source of the country's so-called "illegal immigration crisis" and want to limit the number of immigrant births on U.S. soil. They are calling for changes to jus soli [Latin for "right of the soil"], our birthright citizenship laws. Unfortunately, some Congressional members are listening.

In the last two sessions of Congress, lawmakers introduced the Citizenship Reform Act, which would amend the Immigration and Nationality Act to deny birthright citizenship to children of parents who are neither citizens nor permanent resident aliens. The bill was reintroduced [in January 2007] by Rep. Elton Gallegly, R-Calif, and is pending committee action.

Groups like FAIR assert that immigrant women enter the U.S. to give birth to "anchor babies," who can then sponsor the immigration of other relatives upon reaching the age of 21. They further contend that "anchor babies" and their families create a drain on the country's social service programs. The irrational stance of anti-immigrant advocates echoes that of 1990's welfare reformers. Both assume that childbearing by immigrants or poor women of color creates a cycle of poverty and dependence on the government. Immigrant women and women on welfare are depicted as irresponsible mothers and fraudulent freeloaders.

They're wrong. Several studies have shown that immigrants—documented and undocumented—access social welfare services at much lower rates than U.S.-born citizens. Furthermore, under the 1996 Welfare Reform Act, new immigrants are barred from accessing Medicaid benefits for five years, and sponsor liability rules often render many of these immigrants ineligible for services even after expiration of that restriction. And there is no evidence of intergenerational welfare dependency between immigrant parents and children.

Not surprisingly, pregnant immigrant women have become targets for deportation by immigration officials. On February 7, 2006, Immigration and Customs Enforcement (ICE) officials tried to forcibly deport Jiang Zhen Xing, a Chinese woman pregnant with twins. While her husband and two sons waited for her to complete what should have been a routine interview in a Philadelphia immigration office, ICE officials hustled Mrs. Jiang into a minivan and drove her to New York's JFK airport for immediate deportation back to China. After complaining for hours of severe stomach pains, she was eventually taken to a hospital where doctors found that she had suffered a miscarriage.

## Targeting Pregnant Immigrants

Mrs. Jiang had lived in the U.S. since 1995. Although she entered the country as an undocumented immigrant, she made an agreement with the ICE in 2004 that allowed her to remain in the U.S. as long as she attended routine check-in interviews at a local immigration office. Jiang's case raises an important question: Why would immigration officials be in such a rush to send a pregnant woman back to her country of origin after she had been allowed to stay in the U.S. for over 10 years? Supporters of Mrs. Jiang and other immigrant women targeted while pregnant believe the harassment stems from nativist fears of immigrant mothers giving birth to U.S.-citizen children.

# The Fourteenth Amendment Allows for Dual Citizenship and Divided Loyalties

*Allan Wall*

*During the twentieth century, when it became much easier for people to move around the world thanks to expansions in transportation, and when most countries developed elaborate definitions of citizenship, the complex phenomenon of dual citizenship arose. This is where a single person can claim citizenship, and the rights and privileges that come with it, in two countries rather than one. The issue of dual citizenship, like that of illegal immigration, is one that the framers of the Fourteenth Amendment never took into consideration.*

*In the following selection, author Allan Wall examines the issue of dual citizenship as it pertains to the United States. He notes that, because the Fourteenth Amendment makes it virtually impossible for U.S. citizens to lose their citizenship, foreign nationals and governments have "gamed" the system to make dual citizenship more common. He also wonders whether the rise in the phenomenon has created divided loyalties among some recent immigrant groups. Allan Wall is an Iraq War veteran resident in Mexico, where he works as a university English professor.*

As an American resident in Mexico, I can assure you that U.S. citizenship is seen as a desirable thing.

But I have never heard any Mexican say "I want to become a U.S. citizen because I love the Bill of Rights and I want to be part of a Universal Nation."

Allan Wall, "Memo from Mexico: Shouldn't This Dual Citizenship Thing Be Straightened Out Before We Allow Millions More Immigrants?" VDARE.com, June 21, 2006. Reproduced by permission.

No, most Mexicans who seek American citizenship for themselves or their children do so for personal benefits, and not to become Americans.

When the Mexican government realized it could benefit from this as well, it changed its own citizenship law to allow Mexicans to be dual citizens of both the U.S. and Mexico, for the benefit of Mexico.

In 2003, when the U.S. invaded Iraq, the Mexican government tried to exploit the situation. It announced a census of Mexican citizens (and soldiers of Mexican ancestry) in the U.S. military and negotiation with Saddam Hussein for the release of American prisoners of war who were also Mexican citizens!

Nothing much came of it, but it illustrates the vast possibilities for meddling inherent in widespread dual citizenship.

Does U.S. law allow dual citizenship? You wouldn't get that impression from the oath of citizenship.

When an immigrant becomes a citizen of the United States, he swears an oath of allegiance. Here is what the new citizen promises:

> "I hereby declare, on oath, that I absolutely and entirely renounce and abjure all allegiance and fidelity to any foreign prince, potentate, state, or sovereignty of whom or which I have heretofore been a subject or citizen; that I will support and defend the Constitution and laws of the United States of America against all enemies, foreign and domestic; that I will bear true faith and allegiance to the same; that I will bear arms on behalf of the United States when required by the law; that I will perform noncombatant service in the Armed Forces of the United States when required by the law; that I will perform work of national importance under civilian direction when required by the law; and that I take this obligation freely without any mental reservation or purpose of evasion; so help me God."

But in fact, because of our legislating Supreme Court, dual citizenship is now law of the land.

As the website of the U.S. embassy in Mexico announces to the world:

> "Being a dual national and carrying the passport of another country is perfectly legal. Under U.S. law, naturalizing as a citizen of a foreign state will not in and of itself cause you to lose your U.S. citizenship."

The Selective Service System even exempts some dual citizens from registration.

In the old days, when citizenship meant something, the United States had rules to control this sort of thing. There were "expatriating acts" which could cause you to lose your citizenship.

## Dual Citizenship in Court

Thus Clemente Perez, a U.S.-born citizen of Mexican ancestry, moved to Mexico before World War II and voted in a Mexican election. In *Perez vs. Brownell* (1958) the Supreme Court ruled 5-4 that an American citizen who voted in a foreign election could lose his citizenship.

But a scant nine years later, in the landmark *Afroyim vs. Rusk* case (1967), the court ruled 5-4 that Beys Afroyim, a naturalized citizen, did not renounce his American citizenship by voting in an Israeli election. This invalidated *Perez vs. Brownell*.

U.S. law followed suit (the denaturalization laws were repealed in 1978, since they were a dead letter as soon as the Supreme Court ruled), and now it's almost impossible for an American citizen to lose his citizenship, no matter what he does in a foreign country.

> Would you like to serve in a foreign military? The State Department says that "Military service in foreign countries

usually does not cause loss of citizenship since an intention to relinquish citizenship normally is lacking."

Would you like to run for office in a foreign country? The State Department says that "Currently, there is no general prohibition on U.S. citizens' running for an elected office in a foreign government."

So how could a dual citizen of the U.S. and another country lose his American citizenship?

The State Department has a document entitled *"Possible Loss of U.S. Citizenship and Dual Nationality."* It does list possible expatriating acts—being naturalized in a foreign country, serving as an officer or NCO [non-commissioned officer] in a foreign army, being employed by a foreign government, and even serving in a military engaged in hostile action with the U.S. or being convicted of treason. Yet it adds:

> "the actions listed above can cause loss of U.S. citizenship only if performed voluntarily and with the intention of relinquishing U.S. citizenship. *The Department has a uniform administrative standard of evidence based on the premise that U.S. citizens intend to retain United States citizenship when they obtain naturalization in a foreign state, subscribe to routine declarations of allegiance to a foreign state, or accept non-policy level employment with a foreign government."*

In other words, you can commit a possibly expatriating act and still not lose your citizenship. In fact, the State Department assumes people will do these things and still be U.S. citizens. The key concept is "intent." Even if you say to a foreign government that you're renouncing your U.S. citizenship it doesn't count on the U.S. side unless *intent* to renounce can be proved.

## U.S. Citizenship Is Hard to Lose

Nowadays, the only way to lose American citizenship is by "making a formal renunciation of nationality before a diplomatic or consular officer of the United States *in a foreign state*, in such form as may be prescribed by the Secretary of State."

That's it. That's the *only* way to renounce citizenship.

And practically speaking, it hardly happens anymore. (A rare example is the recent Yaser Hamdi case, involving a dual U.S./Saudi national captured in Afghanistan while serving in the Taliban. Hamdi was a U.S. citizen by virtue of his having been born in the U.S., and as part of his repatriation to Saudi Arabia was required to renounce his U.S. citizenship.)

Today there are millions of dual citizens of the U.S. and other countries. And not only Mexico.

Foreign governments and immigrants are learning more and more ways to leverage dual citizenship and game the system.

Our President and Senate seem determined to increase immigration levels astronomically. But who in our government is dealing with the citizenship question?

Is it wise to open the immigration door even wider, when we haven't really straightened out the citizenship issue?

Shouldn't we clarify citizenship issues (including the anchor baby loophole) *before* we even consider increasing immigration?

Don't all Americans have a stake in the citizenship question—including those of us who are (unfashionable as it may now be) *merely* U.S. citizens?

# Despite an Increase in Dual Citizenship, Most Immigrants Are Loyal to the United States

*Michael Barone*

*In the following selection, conservative columnist and writer Michael Barone argues that dual citizenship presents little threat to an immigrant's loyalty to the United States. He notes in particular that many recent newcomers from Mexico, a country that allows dual citizenship, have served enthusiastically in the U.S. armed forces. Also, he says, most of these and other immigrants are going through the long and often subtle process of assimilation to America that earlier generations of immigrants also experienced.*

*Barone does reject some of the Fourteenth Amendment–based citizenship decisions made by U.S. courts, notably the* Afroyim v. Rusk *decision of 1967, which ensured that an American who voted in a foreign election did not thereby renounce his or her citizenship. Indeed, Barone claims, those who "exercise foreign citizenship" should give up their U.S. citizenship. Nevertheless, and despite the emergence of what he refers to as the rise of "transnational attitudes" among many leaders, most recent immigrants to the United States are completely loyal. Michael Barone has been a staff writer for* U.S. News & World Report *as well as a commentator for Fox News. His writings have also appeared in publications such as the* New York Times *and the* Economist.

I participated today in a panel at the Hudson Institute [a research institute and think tank] on dual citizenship. The subject was Hudson's John Fonte's paper lamenting dual citi-

Michael Barone, "Barone Blog: Dual Citizenship," *U.S. News & World Report*, November 30, 2005. Reprinted with permission.

zenship and urging penalties for U.S. citizens who have foreign citizenship and exercise that citizenship by voting or running for office in foreign elections. . . .

Fonte argues that allowing dual citizenship is a threat to the American tradition of patriotic assimilation.

He argues that the leaders of Mexico and perhaps other countries are engaged in "a sophisticated and long-term strategy similar to the approach promoted by leaders of the European Union and other global and transnational elites, of slowly and steadily building a series of institutions and structures that would lead to a greater and greater political integration in North America—and thus, by definition, a weakening of American constitutional sovereignty."

He notes that the Supreme Court prohibited automatic deprivation of U.S. citizenship for dual citizens who exercise foreign citizenship in *Afroyim v. Rusk*, a 5-to-4 decision that came down in 1967, around the time when we had the lowest percentage of foreign born residents in the 20th century. But he argues that the decision leaves room for laws that penalize those who exercise foreign citizenship and urges that the House include such a provision, sponsored by Arizona Republican J.D. Hayworth, in the immigration and border security legislation it's expected to consider and pass in December.

I was introduced by panel moderator John O'Sullivan as a supporter of more or less open immigration but also a strong supporter of assimilation. I think that's a fair summary of my views, as put forward in my 2001 book, *The New Americans: How the Melting Pot Can Work Again*.

I share Fonte's aversion to dual citizenship. But I don't think, as a practical matter, it poses as great a danger to our country as he does. I am not much troubled that American citizens have served in the military in Israel or have accepted high political posts, up to and including heads of government, in nations like Lithuania. We are in effect re-exporting some of our human capital to places where it is needed and where it can be put to good use. Of course, people who do that should renounce their U.S. citizenship.

## Immigrant Loyalties Are Generally Clear

As for the attempts of the Mexican government to promote a continuing loyalty to Mexico among those who have come to the United States—to the "seventh generation," as Mexican official Juan Hernandez put it (even though Mexico has only existed for a little more than seven generations)—I'm not very worried. I note that despite the drive for dual citizenship, the government of Mexico did not provide for absentee voting in the 2000 presidential election, with the exception of 10 voting stations in border towns that had strictly limited numbers of ballots. The reason was that the PRI [Institutional Revolutionary Party] government evidently feared that most Mexicans in the United States would vote for PAN [the National Action Party]. Mexicans who wanted to vote had to return to Mexico, and when I was there for the 2000 presidential election I actually encountered some, who flew from Austin and Atlanta to Mexico City to cast their ballots for Vicente Fox. Another panelist, Mark Kirkorian of the Center for Immigration Studies, who favors more restrictions on immigration than at present, noted that Mexico is allowing absentee voting for its July 2006 presidential election, but that very few Mexicans in this country have signed up to vote. Juan Hernandez's goal does not seem to be reached for the first generation, much less than seven.

Also, I note that many immigrants, not yet citizens, have volunteered to serve in the United States military forces. Some have been killed and others wounded. Perhaps this can be seen as a cynical attempt to qualify more easily for U.S. citizenship. But I think that service in the U.S. military has to be taken as a pretty serious commitment to the United States.

As for greater and greater political integration in North America, I question how many Mexicans, of whatever citizenship, want that. I remember one day when I was interviewing people in Huntington Park, Calif., and I asked a Mexican man whether he wanted to see the Mexican system of politics and government in the United States. I have seldom seen someone laugh so long and so heartily. The idea was so ridiculous it was funny.

Fonte recalls the attempts of the Italian government to maintain the Italian loyalties of immigrants to America in the 1920s and 1930s. But, as he notes, those attempts failed. Instead, Italian-Americans distinguished themselves by fighting against the Mussolini regime in World War II and in helping to liberate Italy from that regime. I think that Mexican-Americans are not so very different. Yes, Mexico has a border with us. But the Zacatecans Fonte cites have to travel some 2,000 miles to get to Los Angeles. And Italian-Americans regularly traveled back and forth to Italy.

## Transnational Attitudes

So I doubt that Mexican immigrants, even with dual citizenship, are going to dilute by themselves American national sovereignty. Nevertheless, I think I do support Fonte's proposed legislation to penalize acts in furtherance of citizenship of other countries. And I do so because I share his sense that American elites are not sufficiently committed, as Theodore Roosevelt and Woodrow Wilson and Franklin Roosevelt were, to assimilation. Too many of our university, media, corporate, and governmental elites have what Harvard Prof. Samuel Huntington has called transnational attitudes. They think allegiance to any country, but particularly this one, is a sort of noxious prejudice, an outmoded attachment to an unenlightened polity, a primitive and unsophisticated assertion of chauvinism.

The problem is not that immigrants are not prepared to be loyal to the United States. The vast majority of them are. The problem is that too many of our elites think it's tacky to have a special loyalty to the United States. As Fonte pointed out, the immigration laws were revised under Franklin Roosevelt's direction to make it clear that we discouraged dual citizenship. It's interesting that, on this issue, a think tank generally considered conservative should have a panel calling on Americans to return to the example of FDR [Franklin D. Roosevelt].

# Appendices

# Appendix A

## The Amendments to the U.S. Constitution

Amendment I:    Freedom of Religion, Speech, Press, Petition, and
Assembly (ratified 1791)

Amendment II:   Right to Bear Arms (ratified 1791)

Amendment III:  Quartering of Soldiers (ratified 1791)

Amendment IV:   Freedom from Unfair Search and Seizures
(ratified 1791)

Amendment V:    Right to Due Process (ratified 1791)

Amendment VI:   Rights of the Accused (ratified 1791)

Amendment VII:  Right to Trial by Jury (ratified 1791)

Amendment VIII: Freedom from Cruel and Unusual Punishment
(ratified 1791)

Amendment IX:   Construction of the Constitution (ratified 1791)

Amendment X:    Powers of the States and People (ratified 1791)

Amendment XI:   Judicial Limits (ratified 1795)

Amendment XII:  Presidential Election Process (ratified 1804)

Amendment XIII: Abolishing Slavery (ratified 1865)

Amendment XIV:  Equal Protection, Due Process, Citizenship for All
(ratified 1868)

# The Amendments to the U.S. Constitution

Amendment XV:      Race and the Right to Vote (ratified 1870)
Amendment XVI:     Allowing Federal Income Tax (ratified 1913)
Amendment XVII:    Establishing Election to the U.S. Senate
                   (ratified 1913)
Amendment XVIII:   Prohibition (ratified 1919)
Amendment XIX:     Granting Women the Right to Vote (ratified 1920)
Amendment XX:      Establishing Term Commencement for Congress
                   and the President (ratified 1933)
Amendment XXI:     Repeal of Prohibition (ratified 1933)
Amendment XXII:    Establishing Term Limits for U.S. President
                   (ratified 1951)
Amendment XXIII:   Allowing Washington, D.C., Representation in the
                   Electoral College (ratified 1961)
Amendment XXIV:    Prohibition of the Poll Tax (ratified 1964)
Amendment XXV:     Presidential Disability and Succession
                   (ratified 1967)
Amendment XXVI:    Lowering the Voting Age (ratified 1971)
Amendment XXVII:   Limiting Congressional Pay Increases
                   (ratified 1992)

# Appendix B

## Court Cases Relevant to the Fourteenth Amendment's Citizenship Clause

### Scott v. Sanford, 1857
In this case, often referred to as the Dred Scott decision, the Supreme Court ruled that a free black man whose parents were slaves was not a full citizen under the terms of the U.S. Constitution. The decision was soon judged a mistake and was a major inspiration for the Fourteenth Amendment.

### Slaughterhouse Cases, 1873
This was a collection of three cases, concerning the rights of Louisiana slaughterhouses to form an effective monopoly. In it, the Supreme Court decided that the Fourteenth Amendment's citizenship clause governed only national citizenship. It did not, therefore, restrict the right of the state of Louisiana to use its police or other powers.

### Standing Bear v. Crook, 1879
A U.S. District Court case, heard in Omaha, Nebraska, in which the court determined that Standing Bear, a Ponca Indian chief, was a citizen under some of the terms of the Fourteenth Amendment, namely the right to expect due process of law.

### Civil Rights Cases, 1883
A collection of five cases challenging a broad ranging Civil Rights Act passed in 1875. In it the Supreme Court determined that Congress did not have the power under the Fourteenth Amendment to ban racial discrimination on the part of private persons or organizations.

### Elk v. Wilkins, 1884
In this case the Supreme Court determined that a Native American named John Elk could be denied citizenship despite his birth on U.S. soil and his requests for citizenship rights.

He was to be considered, instead, a member of a distinct "foreign" community with which the U.S. Congress maintained treaty relations.

### Plessy v. Ferguson, 1896
In this case the Supreme Court determined that racial segregation was not unconstitutional and that the states therefore had the right to establish institutions that were "separate but equal." The decision provided for an era of "Jim Crow" laws wherein blacks were prohibited from joining whites in contexts as varied as buses and lunch counters. The Court argued that such measures were not a violation of the Fourteenth Amendment because "separate but equal" was a matter of public policy, not the Constitution.

### Korematsu v. United States, 1944
In this case the Supreme Court determined that the Japanese Exclusion Act of 1942 was constitutional. According to the Act, Japanese Americans, even those who were born on U.S. soil, could be removed from areas of the U.S. West Coast that were thought to be militarily vulnerable during World War II. The decision remains highly controversial.

### Perez v. Brownell, 1958
This case ruled that Congress had the right to withdraw an American's citizenship because he had moved to Mexico to avoid military service and had voted in a Mexican election. The ruling was reversed in the 1967 Afroyim v. Rusk decision.

### Trop v. Dulles, 1958
The Supreme Court ruled that an American's citizenship could not be removed by Congress despite the fact that the defendant had deserted the U.S. military in a time of war.

### Saenz v. Roe, 1999
In this case the court decided that an individual state, California, did not maintain the right to limit welfare benefits to newly arrived residents of the state. Such citizens were determined to have the same "privileges and immunities" as long-time residents.

### *Hamdi v. Rumsfeld*, 2004

Yasser Hamdi, a U.S. citizen captured by U.S. military forces in Afghanistan and held as an "enemy combatant," was held to have retained the rights to due process of law that are guaranteed to all American citizens. Most important among these was the right to challenge his detention in court.

# For Further Research

## Books

Alfred Avins, ed., *The Reconstruction Amendments' Debates; the Legislative History and Contemporary Debates in Congress on the 13th, 14th, and 15th Amendments.* Richmond: Virginia Commission on Constitutional Government, 1967.

Judith A. Baer, *Equality Under the Constitution: Reclaiming the Fourteenth Amendment.* Ithaca, NY: Cornell University Press, 1983.

Marion Tinsley, Bennett, *American Immigration Policies.* Washington, DC: Public Affairs Press, 1963.

Raoul Berger, *The Fourteenth Amendment and the Bill of Rights.* Norman: University of Oklahoma Press, 1989.

William Ranulf Brock, *An American Crisis: Congress and Reconstruction, 1865–1867.* London: MacMillan, 1963.

Lee Epstein and Thomas G. Walker, *Constitutional Law for a Changing America: Rights, Liberties, and Justice.* Washington, DC: Congressional Quarterly Press, 1991.

Charles Fairman, Stanley Morrison, and Leonard W. Levy, *The Fourteenth Amendment and the Bill of Rights: The Incorporation Theory.* New York: Da Capo Press, 1970.

George P. Fletcher, *Our Secret Constitution: How Lincoln Redefined American Democracy.* New York: Oxford University Press, 2001.

Lawrence Meir Friedman, *A History of American Law.* 3rd ed. New York: Simon & Schuster, 2005.

Edward P. Hutchinson, *Immigrants and Their Children, 1850–1950.* New York: Wiley, 1956.

Joseph B. James, *The Framing of the Fourteenth Amendment.* Urbana: University of Illinois Press, 1956.

Dale T. Knobel, *"America for the Americans": The Nativist Movement in the United States.* New York: Twayne, 1996.

Beverly Wilson Palmer, ed., *The Selected Papers of Thaddeus Stevens.* Pittsburgh: University of Pittsburgh Press, 1997–1998.

Earl Warren, "The Fourteenth Amendment: Retrospect and Prospect." In *The Fourteenth Amendment: Centennial Volume,* edited by Bernard Schwartz. New York: New York University Press, 1970.

## Periodicals

Sarah A. Adams, "The Basic Right of Citizenship: A Comparative Study." *Center for Immigration Studies,* September 1993. www.cis.org.

Raoul Berger, "Incorporation of the Bill of Rights in the Fourteenth Amendment: A Nine-Lived Cat." *Ohio State Law Journal* 42 (1981).

Katherine Neils Conzen, "Immigrants, Immigrant Neighborhoods, and Ethnic Identity: Historical Issues." *Journal of American History* 66, no. 3 (December 1979).

Charles Fairman, "Does the Fourteenth Amendment Incorporate the Bill of Rights?: The Original Understanding." *Stanford Law Review* 2 (December 1949).

John Raeburn Green, "The Bill of Rights, the Fourteenth Amendment and the Supreme Court." *Michigan Law Review* 46, no. 7 (May 1948).

Louis Henken, "'Selective Incorporation' in the Fourteenth Amendment." *Yale Law Journal* 73, no. 1 (November 1963).

John Higham, "Another Look at Nativism." *Catholic Historical Review* 44 (July 1958).

Robert Pear, "Citizenship Proposal Faces Obstacle in the Constitution." *New York Times*, August 7, 1996.

Tom Shuford, "'Automatic Birthright Citizenship': An Emerging Crisis." *EducationNews.org*, July 25, 2006. www.ednews .org.

"U.S. Mexicans Gain Dual Citizenship." *New York Times*, March 20, 2003.

Ricardo Vargas, "I'm No 'Anchor Baby,' I'm an American." *New America Media*, February 17, 2006. http://news. newamericamedia.org.

## Web Sites

**National Immigration Forum**, www.immigrationforum.org. The Web site of an organization designed "to embrace and uphold America's tradition as a nation of immigrants." It supplies both articles of its own and links to outside sites.

**Federation for American Immigration Reform**, www.fairus .org. The Web site of a group wanting to change immigration laws, including ending the Fourteenth Amendment's guarantee of birthright citizenship.

**The U.S. Constitution Online**, www.usconstitution.net. This Web site provides a wide variety of resources about the Constitution, including explanations of all amendments.

# Index